THE TEN COMMANDMENTS

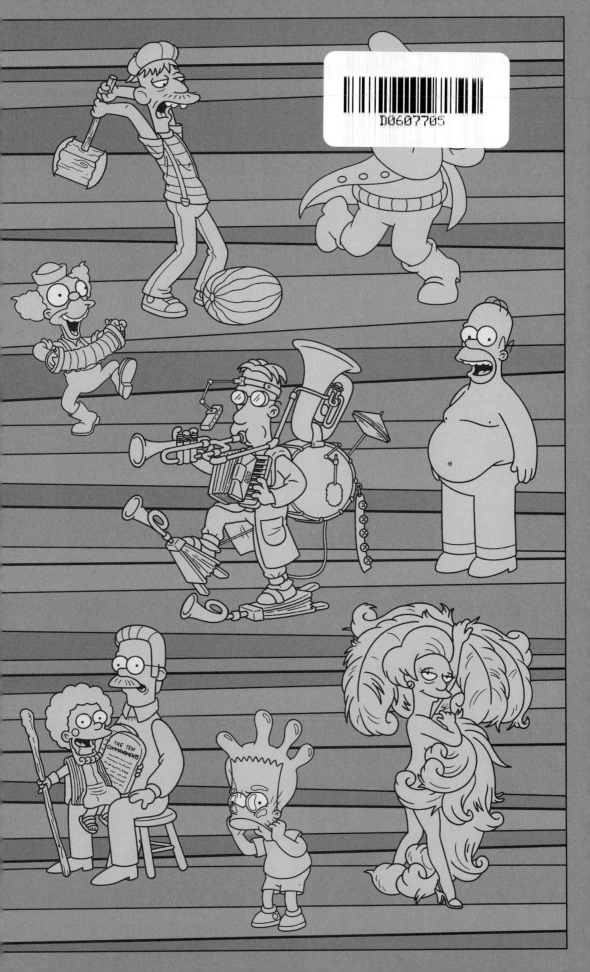

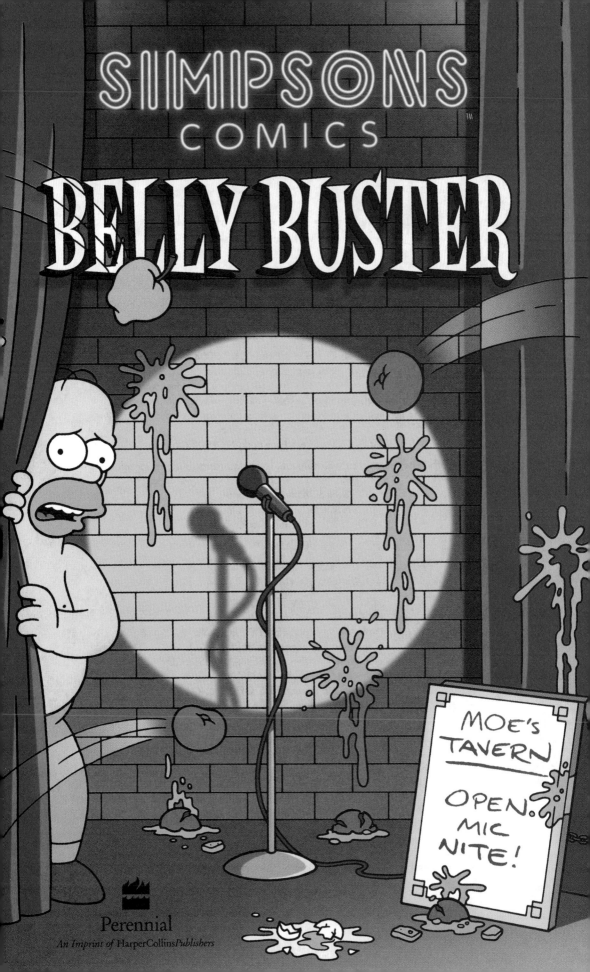

SIMPSONS COMICS
BELLY BUSTER

MOE'S TAVERN

OPEN MIC NITE!

Perennial
An Imprint of HarperCollinsPublishers

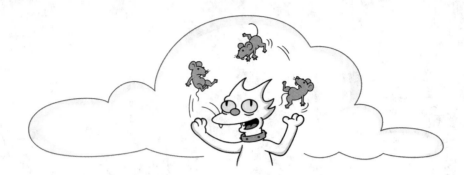

Dedicated to the loving memory of Snowball I:
a feline with great cat skills.

SIMPSONS COMICS BELLY BUSTER

Copyright © 1999, 2000, 2001 & 2004 by
Bongo Entertainment, Inc. All rights reserved.
No part of this book may be used or reproduced in any manner whatsoever
without written permission except in the case of brief quotations
embodied in critical articles and reviews. For information address
HarperCollins Publishers Inc.,
10 East 53rd Street, New York, NY 10022.

HarperCollins books may be purchased for educational, business, or sales
promotional use. For information please write:
Special Markets Department,
HarperCollins Publishers Inc.,
10 East 53rd Street, New York, NY 10022.

FIRST EDITION

ISBN 0-06-058750-4
04 05 06 07 08 QWM 10 9 8 7 6 5 4 3 2 1

Publisher: MATT GROENING
Creative Director: BILL MORRISON
Managing Editor: TERRY DELEGEANE
Director of Operations: ROBERT ZAUGH
Special Projects Art Director: SERBAN CRISTESCU
Art Director: NATHAN KANE
Production Manager: CHRISTOPHER UNGAR
Legal Guardian: SUSAN A. GRODE

Trade Paperback Concepts and Design: SERBAN CRISTESCU

Contributing Artists:

EDWIN AGUILAR, KAREN BATES, TIM BAVINGTON, JEANNINE BLACK, JOHN COSTANZA, DAN DECARLO,
MIKE DECARLO, NATHAN HAMILL, TIM HARKINS, CHRIS HARMON, JASON HO, NATHAN KANE,
TOM KING, JAMES LLOYD, OSCAR GONZÁLEZ LOYO, SCOTT MCRAE, BILL MORRISON, KEVIN M. NEWMAN,
PHIL ORTIZ, MIKE ROTE, SCOTT SHAW!, STEVE STEERE JR., CHRIS UNGAR, ART VILLANUEVA

Contributing Writers:

NEIL ALSIP, IAN BOOTHBY, BRENT FLETCHER, SCOTT M. GIMPLE, GEORGE GLADIR, STEVE LUCHSINGER,
TIM MAILE, JESSE LEON MCCANN, BILLY RUBENSTEIN, SCOTT SHAW!, DOUG TUBER

PRINTED IN CANADA

TONITE ONLY!
Simpsons Comics #49
7 Maggie Come Home
29 Lisa Simpson, Storeroom Raider
Simpsons Comics #51
34 What Would Possibly Happen If™ ...Cletus Went to College??
39 Bart and Lisa and Marge and Homer and Maggie (to a Lesser Extent) vs. Thanksgiving!
Simpsons Comics #53
63 The Beer Boys
85 Around Town with Ned Flanders
Simpsons Comics #54
89 Fork It Over
91 Tanks for Nothing
112 Homer vs. the Wallpaper
116 Picture Perfect
Simpsons Comics #55
121 Siege on Evergreen Terrace
143 Duff Daddy!
Simpsons Comics #56
147 Blind Luck
153 The Yes-Man Who Would Be King

BABY TAKES A POWDER!
BONGO COMICS GROUP
SIMPSONS COMICS
#49
US $2.50
CAN $3.50
APPROVED BY THE COMICS CODE AUTHORITY
WHERE'S MAGGIE?
SPRINGFIELD TOWN HALL
ICE CREAM

MAGGIE COME HOME
BURN HER! BURN THE WITCH!
GASP!
SCRIPT IAN BOOTHBY
PENCILS JAMES LLOYD
INKS TIM BAVINGTON
LETTERS JEANNINE BLACK
COLORS & ART SUPERVISION NATHAN KANE
EDITOR BILL MORRISON
SWITCHED AT BIRTH MATT GROENING

BART, PUT DOWN THAT MAGNIFYING GLASS AND MY SERENA, THE TEENAGE WICCAN DOLL!
FINE, THERE'S TOO MANY GIRLS HERE, ANYWAY! IT'S A COOTIE CONVENTION WAITING TO HAPPEN.
YOU HAVEN'T ANSWERED OUR QUESTION, LISA. DO YOU WANT TO JOIN OUR BABY-SITTERS UNION OR NOT?
WHILE I SUPPORT THE IDEA, I FAIL TO SEE WHY EIGHT-YEAR-OLD GIRLS NEED THIS KIND OF SOLIDARITY.
WE HAVE A DENTAL PLAN.
THIS ONLY COVERS BABY TEETH.
YES, IT FORCES THOSE REPRESENTING THEMSELVES AS THE "TOOTH FAIRY" TO GIVE FAIR MARKET VALUE FOR TEETH LEFT UNDER PILLOWS.
I'M NOT SURE.
♪ UNION MEMBERS GET BACKSTAGE PASSES TO THE COREYS 2 MEN ♫ CONCERT. ♪
COREYS 2 MEN
OOOH! COREYS 2 MEN!
I STILL DON'T KNOW.
LISTEN, SOMETIMES IN OUR BUSINESS IT'S GOOD TO HAVE "PROTECTION," IF YOU KNOW WHAT I'M SAYING.
YOU MEAN FROM THE MOB?
WE MEAN PRO-UNION DOCUMENTARY FILMMAKER, MICHAEL MOORE!
AAAH! I'LL SIGN!

BART, DO YOU HAVE ANY IDEA WHY MAGGIE KEEPS CRAWLING INTO THE *AIR DUCT*?
WELL, THERE'S A *SLIGHT POSSIBILITY* SOMEONE MAY HAVE TOLD HER IT LEADS TO *CANDYLAND!*
I SEE HER! MAGGIE! COME ON OUT, SWEETIE!
MAGGIE'S IN THE VENT AGAIN? I'LL NEED A FRESH PACIFIER AND A JUMP ROPE! *STAT!*
PLOOP!
TA-DAA!
MAGGIE! OH, THANK YOU, LISA! YOU'RE *SO* GOOD WITH CHILDREN!
AW, THAT AIN'T SUCH A *BIG CATCH!* I'D THROW IT BACK AND TRY SWITCHIN' YOUR BAIT. GOOD OL' NIGHT CRAWLERS ALWAYS WORKED FOR ME!

CLEAR THE WAY! NO TIME TO TALK! NEW DONUT DAY!
DID YOUR FATHER LOOK DIFFERENT TODAY?
NAH, SAME BALD YELLOW BLUR AS ALWAYS. LIKE A **COMET** MADE OF BUTTER.
HEY, HOMER, WHAT'S GOING ON? IT'S 100 DEGREES IN HERE, AND **YOU'RE** THE ONLY ONE NOT SWEATIN'.
DO'S DON'TS
YEAH, NORMALLY BY THIS TIME YOU'RE ON YOUR **THIRD SHIRT,** AND WE'RE ON OUR **FIFTH** SET OF NOSE PLUGS.
SIMPSON! IRON THAT SHIRT! IT'S ALL **WRINKLY** AND HAS ENTIRELY TOO MUCH **BACK HAIR!**
GASP! THAT'S IT! YOUR SHIRT! IT'S **PAINTED** ON!
HEH, HEH! I GOT THE IDEA WATCHING BART **WHITE OUT** THE TEACHER'S COMMENTS ON HIS REPORT CARD.

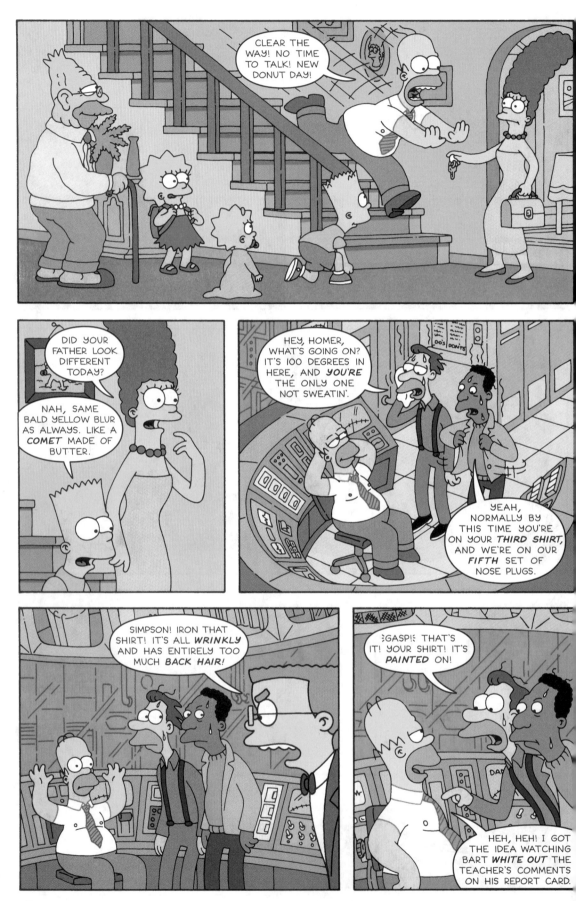

PRETTY SLICK! CAN YOU DO ME?
HEY, YOU BETTER BE CAREFUL! REMEMBER WHAT HAPPENED TO THE FIRST TIN WOODSMAN FROM THE WIZARD OF OZ?
THE ONE WHO WENT *CRAZY* FROM SILVER PAINT POISONING AND TOOK ALL THOSE MUNCHKINS *HOSTAGE* DEMANDING TO SEE THE WIZARD?
YEAH!
PFFT! THAT WAS BECAUSE HE DIDN'T HAVE A *HEART!* NOW STRIP DOWN AND HAND ME THAT PAINT ROLLER.
WOW, THE BABY-SITTERS UNION HAS A *LIMOUSINE* PICK UP AND DROP OFF EACH CHILD! I'M *IMPRESSED!*
BABYSITTER'S LOCAL UNION 203
NO, KELLY! IT'S DAYTIME. WE DON'T NEED TO TURN LIGHTS ON DURING THE DAY!
LIGHTS ON!
LIGHTS ON!
YOU SURE LIKE TURNING ON LIGHTS, DON'T YOU? WELL, I GUESS THEY'LL MAKE IT *EASIER* FOR ME TO READ WHILE YOU WATCH TV!
WE NOW RETURN TO "KRUSTY'S REALLY UNCOMFORTABLE COUCH."
MAN, THIS COUCH IS KILLIN' MY *TUCHUS!*
TRY *NOT SITTING* ON YOUR PUPPETEER, FATSO!

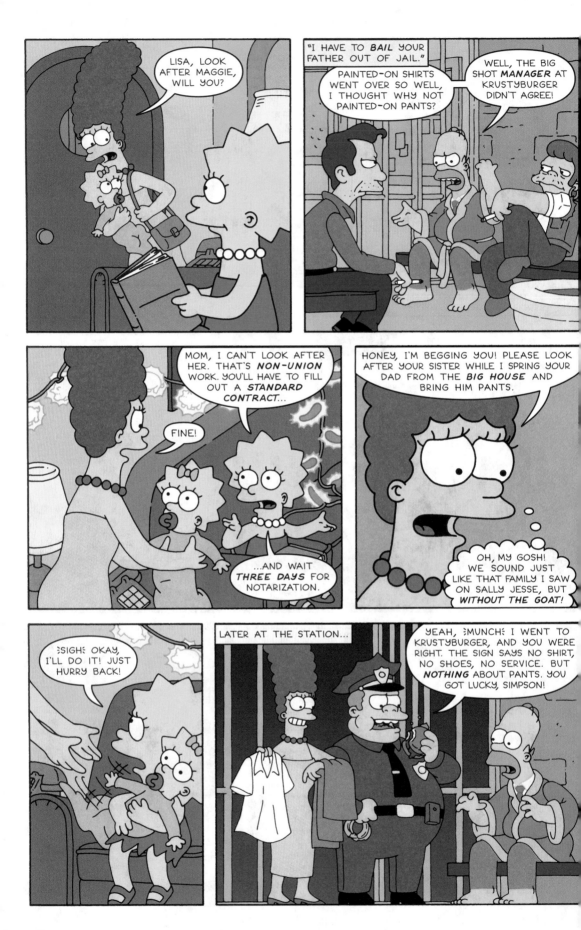

LISA, LOOK AFTER MAGGIE, WILL YOU?

"I HAVE TO *BAIL* YOUR FATHER OUT OF JAIL."

PAINTED-ON SHIRTS WENT OVER SO WELL, I THOUGHT WHY NOT PAINTED-ON PANTS?

WELL, THE BIG SHOT *MANAGER* AT KRUSTYBURGER DIDN'T AGREE!

MOM, I CAN'T LOOK AFTER HER. THAT'S *NON-UNION* WORK. YOU'LL HAVE TO FILL OUT A *STANDARD CONTRACT*...

FINE!

...AND WAIT *THREE DAYS* FOR NOTARIZATION.

HONEY, I'M BEGGING YOU! PLEASE LOOK AFTER YOUR SISTER WHILE I SPRING YOUR DAD FROM THE *BIG HOUSE* AND BRING HIM PANTS.

OH, MY GOSH! WE SOUND JUST LIKE THAT FAMILY I SAW ON SALLY JESSE, BUT *WITHOUT THE GOAT!*

≷SIGH≷ OKAY, I'LL DO IT! JUST HURRY BACK!

LATER AT THE STATION...

YEAH, ≷MUNCH≷ I WENT TO KRUSTYBURGER, AND YOU WERE RIGHT. THE SIGN SAYS NO SHIRT, NO SHOES, NO SERVICE. BUT *NOTHING* ABOUT PANTS. YOU GOT LUCKY, SIMPSON!

OLICE
WHAT SHOULD WE DO WITH THE BAIL MONEY?
OOH, LET'S GO TO KRUSTY-BURGER!
OLICE
I REALLY SHOULD GET BACK HOME.
MARGE, IF I DON'T GET BACK ON THE HORSE NOW, I MAY NEVER EAT ANOTHER *TRIPLE CHEESEBURGER* AGAIN!
MEANWHILE...
KNOCK-KNOCK!
CLICK!
HI, LISA. I'M HERE AS YOUR UNION REPRESENTATIVE FOR A FRIENDLY *SURPRISE* VISIT.
AAAAAH!
EXCUSE ME?
UH...I JUST BIT MY TONGUE.
SO THIS IS THE YOUNG LADY YOU'RE BABY-SITTING?
YES!
YOU KNOW, I JUST CAME FROM A HOUSE ON OAK STREET WHERE ONE OF OUR MEMBERS WAS LOOKING AFTER HER *COUSIN* AND DIDN'T HAVE A *CONTRACT.*
GASP! SHAMEFUL!
OH, DON'T WORRY! SHE'LL *NEVER* BABY-SIT ON *THIS* CONTINENT AGAIN.
LISA! I WANT SOME JUICE!
WHO'S *THAT?*
MY FATHER. HE'S TOO *LAZY* TO GET HIS OWN JUICE.
BUT HIS VOICE IS SO *HIGH!*
HE WORKS PART-TIME AS A CLOWN, MAKING BALLOON ANIMALS FOR SICK KIDS. THERE WAS A DANGEROUS *HELIUM LEAK,* AND HE HAD TO SWALLOW A WHOLE *TANKFUL* OF THE STUFF TO *SAVE* THEM.

WELL, ANYWAY, HERE'S YOUR MEMBERSHIP CARD. IT WAS NICE MEETING YOU MEMBER 203-24.
WANDA, WE'VE BEEN IN THE SAME CLASS SINCE ***KINDERGARTEN***!
HI, LISA! THANKS AGAIN!
HI, MOM! HI, DAD!
DAD?
I MEAN ***DADDY-O!*** THAT'S WHAT WE ***JAZZ*** FANS CALL...
...TOTAL ***STRANGERS*** OUR MOM BRINGS HOME FROM THE BAR.
WOW, JUST LIKE THAT FAMILY ON SALLY JESSE. WELL, HAPPY SITTING!
HI!
HEY, BART! NO TIME TO TALK! FOOTBALL'S ON!
YES, I'VE MADE THE ROUNDS. EVERYTHING'S IN PERFECT ORDER. OH, ONE ***SMALL*** CORRECTION.
THE KID LISA SIMPSON IS BABY-SITTING IS A ***BLOND***, NOT A REDHEAD. YEAH, SHE'S WEARING A ***BLUE*** "SWEE' PEA" STYLE ***OUTFIT***.

AFTER ALL THAT STRESS, I THINK WE CAN USE SOME CHOCOLATE-FLAVORED SOYMILK.
SOY MILK
THE DIFFERENCE IS THE AFTERTASTE!
ANOTHER **TOUCHDOWN** FOR SHELBYVILLE!
D'OH!
KNOCK-KNOCK!
D'OH!
COME IN!
I'M HERE FOR THE GIRL LISA SIMPSON IS SITTING.
SHE **FITS** THE DESCRIPTION.
TAKE HER!
HOMER! A LIMOUSINE JUST **DROVE OFF** WITH **MAGGIE** IN THE BACK!
RELAX, MARGE. MAYBE SHE JUST WON AN AWARD. NOW THINK, WHAT WAS SHE **NOMINATED** FOR?
WHAT? A LIMO? **NOOOO!**
SO YOU SEE, MS. SINCLAIR, IT WAS ALL A **BIG** MISUNDERSTANDING. IF I CAN JUST GET MY SISTER **BACK**, WE'LL BE ON OUR WAY.
Baby-Sitters Local 203
I **WISH** IT WERE THAT SIMPLE.

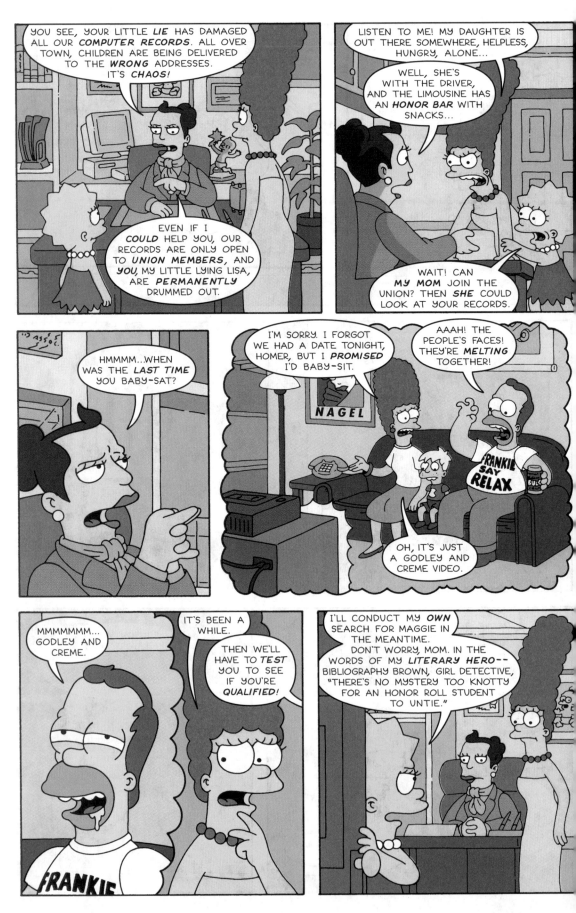

YOU SEE, YOUR LITTLE *LIE* HAS DAMAGED ALL OUR *COMPUTER RECORDS*. ALL OVER TOWN, CHILDREN ARE BEING DELIVERED TO THE *WRONG* ADDRESSES. IT'S *CHAOS!*

EVEN IF I *COULD* HELP YOU, OUR RECORDS ARE ONLY OPEN TO *UNION MEMBERS*, AND *YOU*, MY LITTLE LYING LISA, ARE *PERMANENTLY* DRUMMED OUT.

LISTEN TO ME! MY DAUGHTER IS OUT THERE SOMEWHERE, HELPLESS, HUNGRY, ALONE...

WELL, SHE'S WITH THE DRIVER, AND THE LIMOUSINE HAS AN *HONOR BAR* WITH SNACKS...

WAIT! CAN *MY MOM* JOIN THE UNION? THEN *SHE* COULD LOOK AT YOUR RECORDS.

HMMMM...WHEN WAS THE *LAST TIME* YOU BABY-SAT?

I'M SORRY. I FORGOT WE HAD A DATE TONIGHT, HOMER, BUT I *PROMISED* I'D BABY-SIT.

OH, IT'S JUST A GODLEY AND CREME VIDEO.

AAAH! THE PEOPLE'S FACES! THEY'RE *MELTING* TOGETHER!

NAGEL

FRANKIE SAY RELAX

MMMMMMM... GODLEY AND CREME.

IT'S BEEN A WHILE.

THEN WE'LL HAVE TO *TEST* YOU TO SEE IF YOU'RE *QUALIFIED!*

FRANKIE

I'LL CONDUCT MY *OWN* SEARCH FOR MAGGIE IN THE MEANTIME. DON'T WORRY, MOM. IN THE WORDS OF MY *LITERARY HERO*-- BIBLIOGRAPHY BROWN, GIRL DETECTIVE, "THERE'S NO MYSTERY TOO KNOTTY FOR AN HONOR ROLL STUDENT TO UNTIE."

ARE YOU SURE YOU HAVE THE RIGHT PLACE? I WAS KINDA EXPECTING RALPH.
FOR COMPLAINTS, DIAL THE 1-900 NUMBER ON THE BACK OF THE DIAPER.
MAN, THAT'S $4.99 A MINUTE! TELL YOU WHAT, LITTLE GUY, LET'S THINK ABOUT WHAT TO DO OVER A NICE GRILLED CHEESE SANDWICH.
HMMMMM... OUTTA BREAD. WHAT WOULD MARTHA STEWART DO? HEY, I'LL BET SHE'D USE TWO SLABS OF THIS HARDENED BACON FAT!
GZZZZZXXX! SNORK!
FWOOOSH!
FIRE! MY GOD! I MUSTA DOZED OFF! I'M PARALYZED WITH FEAR! IS THIS THE END OF CHIEF CLANCY WIGGUM?
EMERGENCY NUMBERS
1 2 3 4 5 6 7 8 9 * 0 #

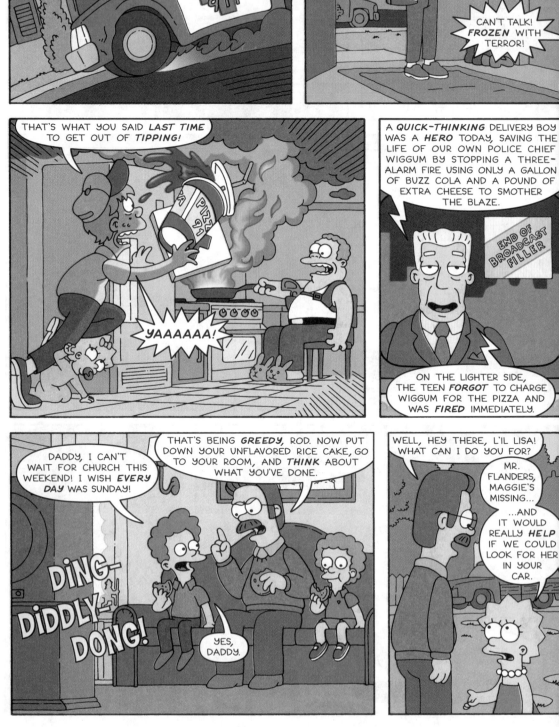

SKRREEEEECH!

HELLO? CHIEF WIGGUM? I HAVE YOUR *USUAL* EXTRA-LARGE HOG BUTCHER'S SUPREME PIZZA AND SUPER-SLAKER-SIZED SODA!

CAN'T TALK! *FROZEN* WITH TERROR!

THAT'S WHAT YOU SAID *LAST TIME* TO GET OUT OF *TIPPING!*

YAAAAAA!

A *QUICK-THINKING* DELIVERY BOY WAS A *HERO* TODAY, SAVING THE LIFE OF OUR OWN POLICE CHIEF WIGGUM BY STOPPING A THREE-ALARM FIRE USING ONLY A GALLON OF BUZZ COLA AND A POUND OF EXTRA CHEESE TO SMOTHER THE BLAZE.

END OF BROADCAST FILLER

ON THE LIGHTER SIDE, THE TEEN *FORGOT* TO CHARGE WIGGUM FOR THE PIZZA AND WAS *FIRED* IMMEDIATELY.

DADDY, I CAN'T WAIT FOR CHURCH THIS WEEKEND! I WISH *EVERY DAY* WAS SUNDAY!

THAT'S BEING *GREEDY*, ROD. NOW PUT DOWN YOUR UNFLAVORED RICE CAKE, GO TO YOUR ROOM, AND *THINK* ABOUT WHAT YOU'VE DONE.

DING-DIDDLY-DONG!

YES, DADDY.

WELL, HEY THERE, L'IL LISA! WHAT CAN I DO YOU FOR?

MR. FLANDERS, MAGGIE'S MISSING...

...AND IT WOULD REALLY *HELP* IF WE COULD LOOK FOR HER IN YOUR CAR.

WELL, NOW HERE'S THE THING, LISA. ALL THE MAJOR RELIGIONS OF THE WORLD KINDA UNIONIZED LAST YEAR, AND MUCH AS I'D LIKE TO, I CAN'T HELP A SCAB LIKE YOU.
LOCAL 666?
LOCAL 666
YES, NOT THE BEST NUMBER. IF ONLY WE CHRISTIANS HAD GOTTEN THERE A LITTLE EARLIER OR A LITTLE LATER. WE TRIED TO TRADE NUMBERS WITH THE BUDDHISTS, BUT THEY WOULDN'T GO FOR IT.
BUT I REALLY NEED YOUR HELP.
LOCAL 666
NO CAN DO, LISA. NOT WITHOUT RISKING MY MEDICAL PLAN...
...AND FACING ETERNAL DAMNATION. SORRY, IT'S A REAL STRICT UNION.
I HOPE MOM'S DOING BETTER THAN I AM.
BRAVO, MRS. SIMPSON! NOT ONLY DID YOU BATHE AND DIAPER YOUR CHILD, BUT IN YOUR EXTRA TIME YOU HAVE TAUGHT IT TO PLAY THE BANJO!
THE REST OF YOU SHOULD HANG YOUR PRE-TEEN HEADS IN SHAME!

A BABY? BUT I'M SURE I ORDERED A NEW CASE OF PICKLED CLAMS!
LOOK, WE DON'T MAKE MISTAKES.
ER, ASIDE FROM THAT ONE EARLIER TODAY AT THE WIGGUM PLACE. ANYWAY, I WAS TOLD TO PICK HER UP AND BRING HER HERE.
EXIT
HEY! IT'S ONE OF THOSE EENIE-BEANIE BABIES! CAN I HOLD IT MOE? I WON'T RIP OFF THE TAG!
YEAH, WHATEVER! JUST LOOK AFTER HER WHILE I FRESHEN UP THIS OLD CLAM BRINE!
WOW! IT'S REALLY LIFELIKE!
BATHROOMS
DRINK Duff
WHOA! THE DOLL'S ATTACKING ME, LIKE THE DOLL THAT ATTACKED PEOPLE IN THE MOVIE, "VALLEY OF THE DOLLS"!
WHAAAAAAAA!
SPLOOSH!
GGGLP! GLUG!
FWAP!

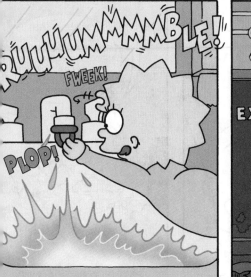

RUUUUMMMMBLE!

FWEEK!

PLOP!

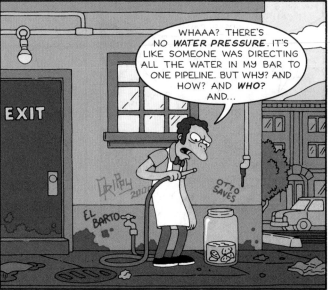

WHAAA? THERE'S NO *WATER PRESSURE*. IT'S LIKE SOMEONE WAS DIRECTING ALL THE WATER IN MY BAR TO ONE PIPELINE. BUT WHY? AND HOW? AND *WHO*? AND...

EXIT

EL BARTO

OTTO SAVES

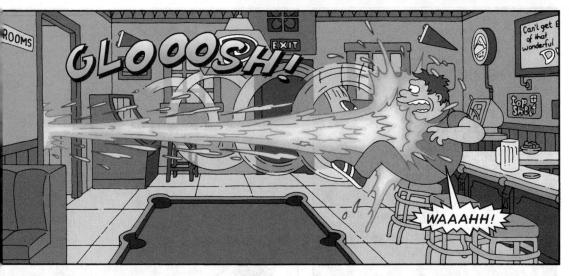

GLOOOSH!

ROOMS

EXIT

Can't get enough of that wonderful D

top shelf

WAAAHH!

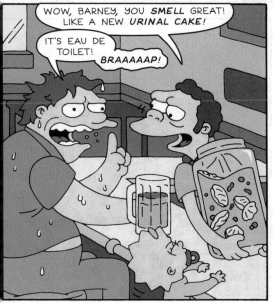

WOW, BARNEY, YOU *SMELL* GREAT! LIKE A NEW *URINAL CAKE*!

IT'S EAU DE TOILET! *BRAAAAAP!*

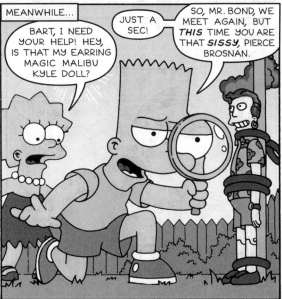

MEANWHILE...

BART, I NEED YOUR HELP! HEY, IS THAT MY EARRING MAGIC MALIBU KYLE DOLL?

JUST A SEC!

SO, MR. BOND, WE MEET AGAIN, BUT *THIS* TIME YOU ARE THAT *SISSY*, PIERCE BROSNAN.

MAGGIE'S GONE, AND IT'S ALL MY FAULT! I CAN'T GET INTO THE COMPUTER RECORDS BECAUSE--
WAIT! YOU'RE SAYING I'M 100% BLAME-FREE AND YOU'RE THE ONE IN TROUBLE?
YES, BUT...!
WAIT! I'M SAVORING THE MOMENT!
BART!
OKAY! OKAY! WE CAN SEARCH FOR THE INFO YOU NEED AT MILHOUSE'S DAD'S APARTMENT. HE'S GOT A NEW COMPUTER!
YEAH, ALL THE APARTMENTS IN THIS SINGLES COMPLEX GET THE INTERNET FOR FREE!
UM...DAD, ALL WE CAN GET IS THIS DATING WEB PAGE.
OH, THAT CAME ALREADY LOADED. I'VE NEVER USED IT! HEH, HEH!
WELL, IT APPEARS THAT ONE OF US DOES NOT KNOW HOW TO FILL OUT A SIMPLE CYBERDATE FORM.
OKAY, LET'S CROSS-REFERENCE THE NAME MAGGIE WITH ALL KNOWN SITTER SITES AND RUN A UNIX SCAN OVER THE DOS BASE.
MILHOUSE, ARE YOU MAKING ALL THAT UP TO IMPRESS ME?
YES, MA'AM.
GIMME THAT KEYBOARD!

KLICK!
KLICKETY-KLACK!
KLACK!
OH, MY GOSH! LOOK WHO'S THE REAL HEAD OF THE BABY-SITTER'S UNION! IT ALL MAKES SENSE NOW!
IT DOES?
HEY, DOES THAT BABY-SITTER SITE LIST ANY HOT SINGLE MOMS?
DAD!
WAIT, LIS, I DON'T GET IT.
LET'S GO! I'LL EXPLAIN ON THE WAY!
MEANWHILE, AT BABY-SITTER'S LOCAL 203...
MOE'S
THIS IS KENT BROCKMAN, LIVE AT MOE'S TAVERN, WHERE YET ANOTHER MEDICAL EMERGENCY HAS OCCURRED. TWO ON-DUTY POLICEMEN STOPPED IN AT THE BAR FOR A FEW BEERS EARLIER TODAY, ONLY TO FIND THE PROPRIETOR AND ONE OF HIS CUSTOMERS SEVERELY NAUSEOUS. THE CULPRIT--CLAMS GONE BAD!
OH, MY LORD! THAT'S MAGGIE!
MARGE, WAIT! YOU PASSED THE TEST! I WAS JUST GOING TO SWEAR YOU IN!
I COULD USE THE $2.50 AN HOUR, BUT RIGHT NOW I'VE GOT TO GET MY BABY!

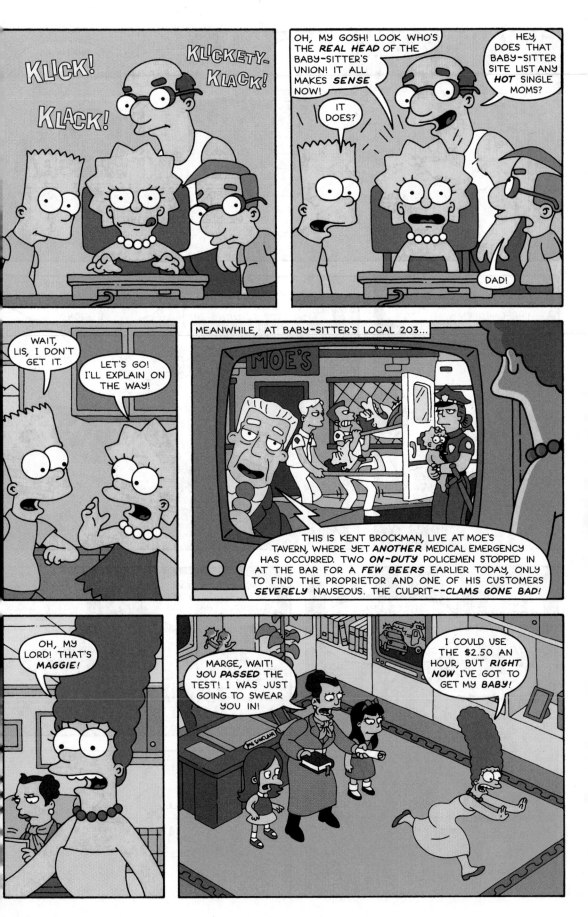

FREEZE, SCUMBAGS!
THE JIG IS UP, BURNS!
AAAH! CHILDREN! I THOUGHT WE SPRAYED FOR THOSE, SMITHERS!
THAT WAS FOR STINKBUGS, SIR!
SO, YOU KNOW I PLANTED SUBLIMINAL MESSAGE TAPES IN THE UNION LIMOUSINES TO MAKE THE CHILDREN WANT TO WASTE ELECTRICITY?
THAT'S WHY KELLY WOULDN'T STOP TURNING ON EVERY LIGHT IN THE HOUSE.
YES, SOON I'D HAVE RAISED A GENERATION OF ENERGY WASTERS, AND I'D FINALLY BE RICH!
BUT YOU'RE ALREADY RICH!
OH, YES, I HAVE BAZILLIONS, BUT THE GAZILLIONAIRES STILL LAUGH AT ME FROM THEIR DIAMOND TOWERS.
MAN, IT WAS EVIL, BUT I GOTTA HAND IT TO YOU. THAT WAS A GOOD PLAN!
YES, AND I WOULD HAVE GOTTEN AWAY WITH IT TOO, IF IT WASN'T FOR YOU KIDS AND THAT DOG.
BUT WE DIDN'T BRING A DOG.

OH, THAT MUST BE ONE OF *MINE* THEN. I SUGGEST YOU START RUNNING FOR YOUR LIVES.
GRRRRR!
AAAAA!
AAAAA!
YAAAA!
SOON...
WELL, I JUST THANK HEAVEN THAT WE GOT MAGGIE BACK *SAFE* AND *SOUND*. I *APPRECIATE* ALL YOU TRIED TO DO.
BUT WHERE'S MILHOUSE?
OH, UM...HE'S...
"...GONE TO A *BETTER PLACE*."

AAAR! STOP 'YER BLUBBERIN'! I SAID WOMEN SIGNED UP FOR THE CRUISE. BUT **NO REFUNDS** BE THE LAW OF THE SEA.
AT LEAST WE GET TO GO TO **HAWAII!**
WHAT'S THAT, HANDSOME PETE?
PSSST MNMRR WOONA FUZAGER...
OH! GAAAR!
I'M AFRAID WE ONLY HAVE ENOUGH FUEL TO GET TO **LEPER ISLAND**!
AWWWWW!
SO WHAT HAPPENED TO THE BABY-SITTER'S UNION?
IT WAS **DISBANDED** BY THE AUTHORITIES. MS. SINCLAIR AND THE GIRLS WHO WERE IN ON BURNS'S PLAN ARE BEING **FORCED** TO RETAKE BABY-SITTER TRAINING.
"THE BEST PART IS, THEY'RE DOING THEIR TRAINING AT A **DAYCARE CENTER** THAT PROVIDES **LOW-COST CARE** FOR THE CHILDREN OF **SINGLE WORKING MOTHERS**."
WELL, THAT'S GOOD. I SUPPOSE MR. BURNS GOT AWAY WITH HIS **SCHEME** AS USUAL.
OH, NO...

"...HE AND MR. SMITHERS HAVE THE NIGHT SHIFT!"
BLAST IT, BABY! STOP FLICKING THAT LIGHT ON AND OFF IN MY EYES!
:SIGH: YOU'D MAKE A WONDERFUL MOTHER, SIR!
BOOKS
THE END

#1
LISA SIMPSON,
STOREROOM RAIDER
WHAT MUTANT HORRORS LURK IN...
...THE CLASSROOM THAT SCHOOL FORGOT?!
GROENING
J.Ho

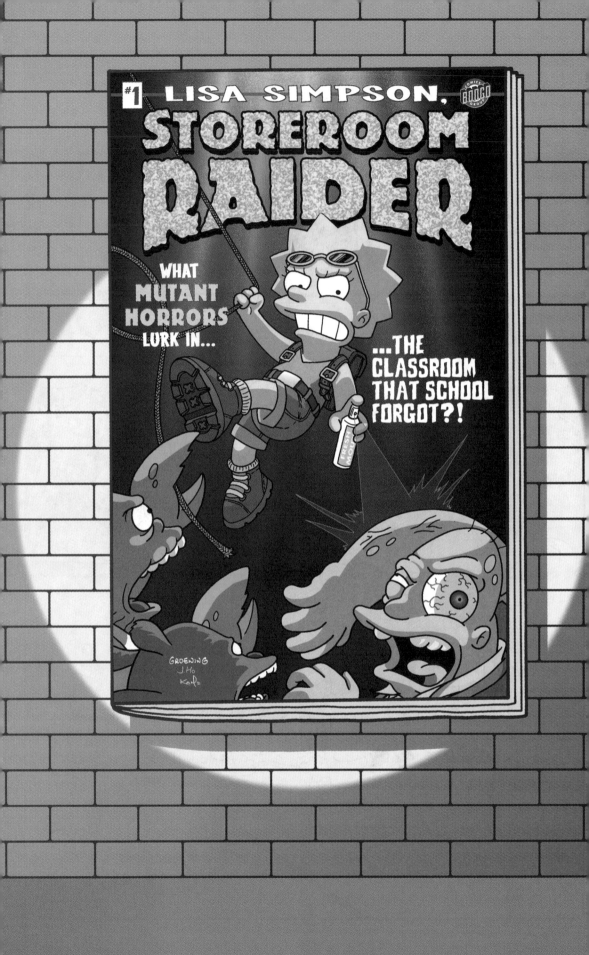

LISA SIMPSON, STOREROOM RAIDER
MUTANTS. GIANT KILLER HAMSTERS. I'D BETTER GET EXTRA CREDIT FOR THIS.
CRAK!
MISS HOOVER'S CLASS, SPRINGFIELD ELEMENTARY SCHOOL.
WELL, THAT'S THE LAST OF THE WHITE OUT. THERE'S NO CHOICE BUT TO SEND ONE OF YOU TO THE STOREROOM FOR CHALK.
BUT MS. HOOVER, YOU'VE ALREADY SENT RALPH AND JANEY, AND NEITHER HAS COME BACK.
SO YOU'RE VOLUNTEERING? GREAT. TAKE YOUR KNAPSACK AND BRING BACK SOME ERASERS WHILE YOU'RE THERE.
IT'S ODD. I CAN SEE RALPH GETTING LOST ON HIS WAY TO THE STOREROOM, BUT JANEY'S A JR. PATHMAKER SCOUT.
IT'S EMPTY! WHERE ARE ALL THE SCHOOL SUPPLIES? ARE THE REPUBLICANS BACK IN POWER?
MAYBE THERE'S SOMETHING IN THAT DARK FOREBODING CORNER.
CHALK ERASERS
AAAAAAAAAAH!!

OKAY, IT'S DARK. I'M UNDERGROUND. SURROUNDED. WHAT WOULD HARRIET THE SPY DO?
AAAAAAAAAAH!
CLAP!
COUGH!
CHOKE!
IS THAT JANEY'S HAIR RIBBON?
SHE'S USING HER PATHMAKER TRAINING TO MARK A TRAIL!
BACK! GET BACK!
LUCKY I HAD THESE KRUSTY FROOT BY THE KILOMETER™ ROLL UPS IN MY BACKPACK.
CRAK!
THEY ONLY WANT YOUR FRUITY WHIP.
AAAAAAH!
OKAY, THAT'S IT! I'M TIRED OF SCREAMING! MY THROAT'S RAW!
WHO ARE YOU? WHAT ARE THEY?
BRRRRRRING!
COME NOW. YOU'RE LATE.
LATE FOR WHAT?

CLASS!
HI LISA!
WAY TO NOT ESCAPE AND GET HELP, LISA!
YOU'RE *TEACHERS*?
SUBSTITUTES. BUT THE STUDENTS JUST *WOULDN'T* LISTEN, SO WE TOOK THE SCHOOL'S HAMSTERS AND FLED UNDERGROUND, WHERE IT WAS *SAFE*.
BUT HOW DO YOU *LIVE*?
WE STEAL SUPPLIES FROM THE STOREROOM AND DRINK THE SWEET, SWEET WATER THAT FLOWS FROM ABOVE.
EW! WE'RE RIGHT UNDER *THE NUCLEAR POWER PLANT*. THAT EXPLAINS THE MUTATIONS AND GIANT HAMSTERS.
BUT WHY DO YOU WANT RALPH, JANEY AND ME?
WHAT ARE TEACHERS WITHOUT *STUDENTS*? PREVIOUSLY WE TAUGHT THE HAMSTERS, BUT THEY'RE STUCK AT A *GRADE ONE* READING LEVEL.
Go Dog Go
NOW, WITH YOU ALL HERE, WE ARE *COMPLETE*.
WELL, *I* WANTED TO GET *CABLE* TOO, BUT FREDERICKS HERE THINKS TV IS TOO *LOWBROW*.
MUST WE *ALWAYS* FIGHT IN FRONT OF COMPANY?

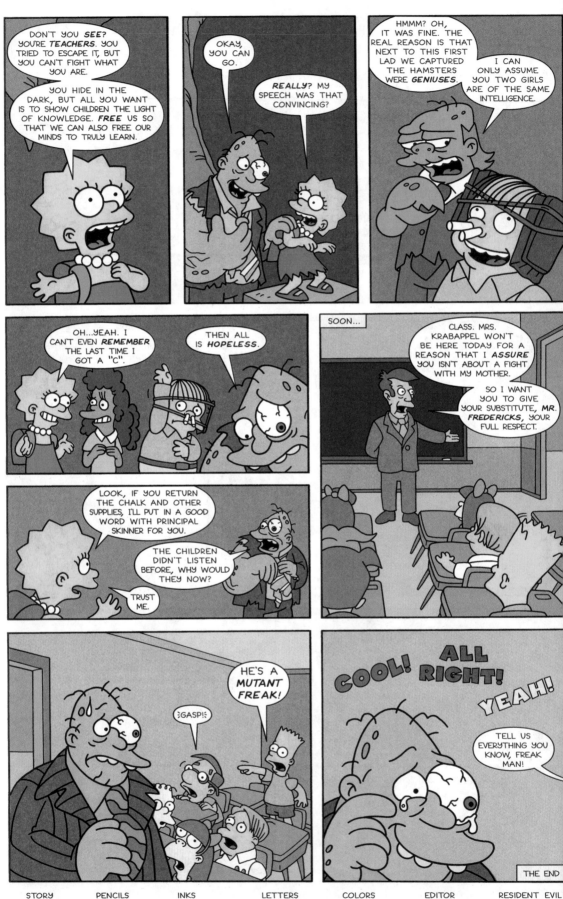

STORY
IAN BOOTHBY

PENCILS
TOM KING

INKS
STEVE STEERE, JR.

LETTERS
CHRIS UNGAR

COLORS
NATHAN KANE

EDITOR
BILL MORRISON

RESIDENT EVIL
MATT GROENING

WHAT WOULD POSSIBLY HAPPEN IF™
BONGO COMICS GROUP
$2.50 US
$3.50 CAN
1
WHAT WOULD POSSIBLY HAPPEN IF™
HEY, MAW! PASS ME THE CAT!
CLETUS™
WENT TO COLLEGE?
CLETUS, YOU'RE THE KING! FILLIN' THE DEAN'S HOUSE WITH GOATS-- WHAT A GAG!
THEY ONLY GONNA MAKE YOU GAG IF YOU DON'T SKIN 'EM FIRST!
U
ACME GOAT FEED
GROENING

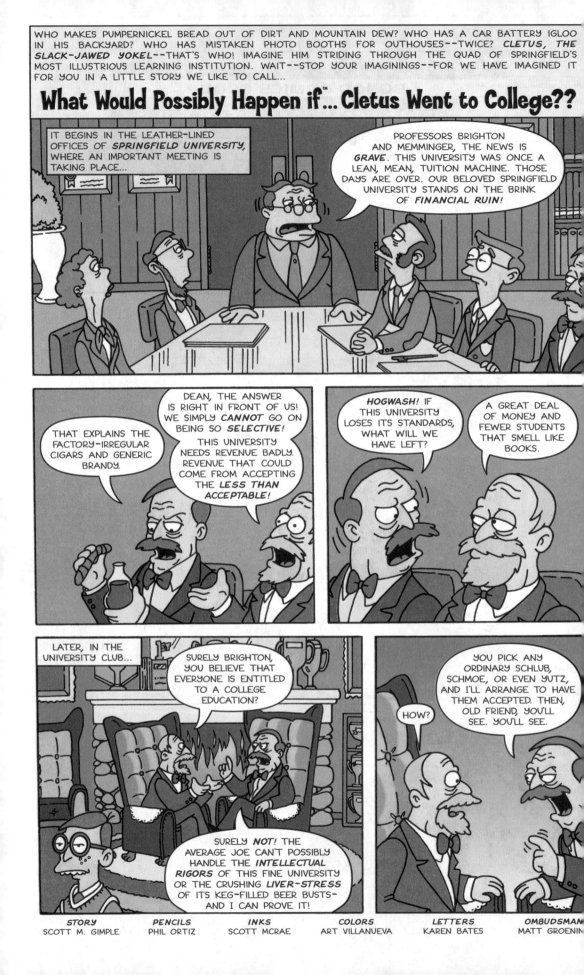

WHO MAKES PUMPERNICKEL BREAD OUT OF DIRT AND MOUNTAIN DEW? WHO HAS A CAR BATTERY IGLOO IN HIS BACKYARD? WHO HAS MISTAKEN PHOTO BOOTHS FOR OUTHOUSES--TWICE? *CLETUS, THE SLACK-JAWED YOKEL*--THAT'S WHO! IMAGINE HIM STRIDING THROUGH THE QUAD OF SPRINGFIELD'S MOST ILLUSTRIOUS LEARNING INSTITUTION. WAIT--STOP YOUR IMAGININGS--FOR WE HAVE IMAGINED IT FOR YOU IN A LITTLE STORY WE LIKE TO CALL...

What Would Possibly Happen if™... Cletus Went to College??

IT BEGINS IN THE LEATHER-LINED OFFICES OF *SPRINGFIELD UNIVERSITY*, WHERE AN IMPORTANT MEETING IS TAKING PLACE...

PROFESSORS BRIGHTON AND MEMMINGER, THE NEWS IS *GRAVE*. THIS UNIVERSITY WAS ONCE A LEAN, MEAN, TUITION MACHINE. THOSE DAYS ARE OVER. OUR BELOVED SPRINGFIELD UNIVERSITY STANDS ON THE BRINK OF *FINANCIAL RUIN*!

DEAN, THE ANSWER IS RIGHT IN FRONT OF US! WE SIMPLY *CANNOT* GO ON BEING SO *SELECTIVE*! THIS UNIVERSITY NEEDS REVENUE BADLY. REVENUE THAT COULD COME FROM ACCEPTING THE *LESS THAN ACCEPTABLE*!

THAT EXPLAINS THE FACTORY-IRREGULAR CIGARS AND GENERIC BRANDY.

HOGWASH! IF THIS UNIVERSITY LOSES ITS STANDARDS, WHAT WILL WE HAVE LEFT?

A GREAT DEAL OF MONEY AND FEWER STUDENTS THAT SMELL LIKE BOOKS.

LATER, IN THE UNIVERSITY CLUB...

SURELY BRIGHTON, YOU BELIEVE THAT EVERYONE IS ENTITLED TO A COLLEGE EDUCATION?

SURELY *NOT!* THE AVERAGE JOE CAN'T POSSIBLY HANDLE THE *INTELLECTUAL RIGORS* OF THIS FINE UNIVERSITY OR THE CRUSHING *LIVER-STRESS* OF ITS KEG-FILLED BEER BUSTS- AND I CAN PROVE IT!

YOU PICK ANY ORDINARY SCHLUB, SCHMOE, OR EVEN YUTZ, AND I'LL ARRANGE TO HAVE THEM ACCEPTED. THEN, OLD FRIEND, YOU'LL SEE. YOU'LL SEE.

HOW?

STORY	*PENCILS*	*INKS*	*COLORS*	*LETTERS*	*OMBUDSMAN*
SCOTT M. GIMPLE	PHIL ORTIZ	SCOTT MCRAE	ART VILLANUEVA	KAREN BATES	MATT GROENIN

HOW ABOUT A LITTLE WAGER? SAY, FOR THAT GARRISON KEILLOR LAKE WOBEGON WASH BASIN OF YOURS?
DONE! A BET IT IS!
BUT WHERE WILL WE FIND THIS SHRUGGING JOE BISQUICK?
I SAY IF WE ARE LOOKING FOR THE MOST COMMON MAN, LET US GO TO THE MOST COMMON PLACE!
MICHIGAN?
CLOSE! BUT I WAS THINKING...
..."THE SPRINGFIELD MUNICIPAL DUMP!"
WELL, LOOKY HERE, I GOTS ME A NEW GLASS EYE!
SEE HIM, MEMMINGER? NARY A DROP OF KNOWLEDGE HAS EVER BEEN ABSORBED BY HIS PRIMITIVE HOMO-GILLIGAN MIND. HE'S PERFECT! SHOW ME HOW HE COULD POSSIBLY SURVIVE IN A UNIVERSITY SETTING!
OOOH! PINCH ME! PREEVIUSLY-OWNED YOGURT!
HEY, YOU SEEN A GLASS EYE?
UH...I THINK I SAW ONE NEAR THEM CAR BAT-TRIES.

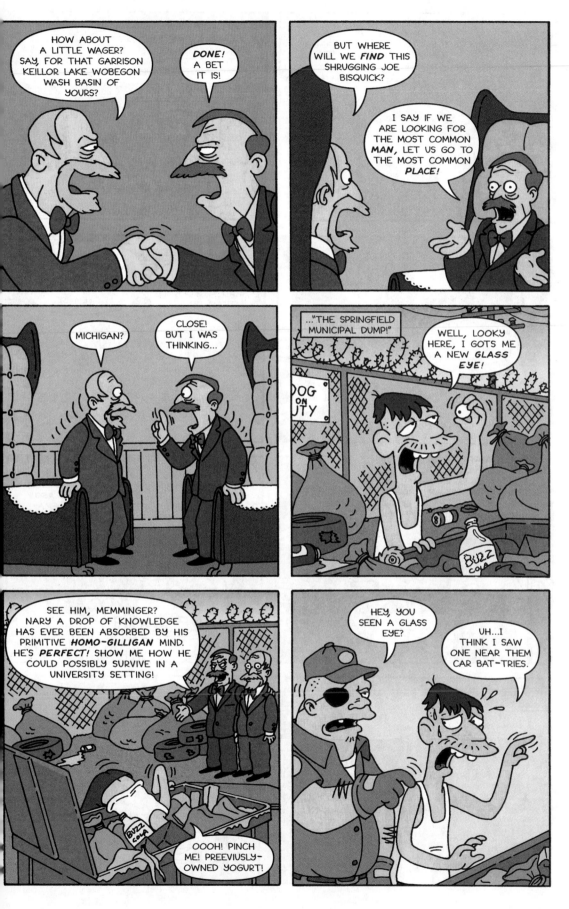

AND SOON...
YOUR MAJOR IS PHILOSOPHY. YOU WILL GRAPPLE WITH THE VERY MEANING OF LIFE ITSELF.
CLETUS, HERE'S A PEN AND A NOTE-BOOK.
WHICH ONE A THEM'S THE NOTEBOOK?
Apathy Club meeting cancelled-- like you care.
AND SO, NIETZCHE BUILT UPON DARWIN'S IDEA OF SURVIVAL OF THE FITTEST, ARRIVING AT HIS IDEA OF THE SUPER...
WHEN'S THE COMMERCIAL? I GOTSTA STOCK THE SEPTIC, IF YOU KNOW WHAT I MEAN.
GOOD GOD! WHO LET THESE PIGS LOOSE IN THE SUPERCOLLIDER??
HIT THAT RED BUTTON. IT COOKS 'EM REAL SWEET.
UM, WHAT IS OUR ALL-AMERICAN ACADEMIC-DEBATE TEAM DOING?
MUD WRESTLING THOSE BOYS FROM YALE. I GOT 'EM STARTED, THEN I LET 'EM BE.
THE FIRE STARTED WHEN THE STILL DONE BLOWED UP. I DONE THOUGHT THAT CHEMISTRY LABORATORIES WAS FIRE-PROOFED.
XXX
XXX
HERE, A BET IS A BET. ALAS, BRIGHTON, PERHAPS I OVER-ESTIMATED THE COMMON MAN.
PERHAPS? HAH! YOU SEE, MEMMINGER, THERE'S A REASON FOR US TO REMAIN SELECTIVE!
SELECTIVE SCHMELECTIVE, GENTLEMEN. WE'RE IN TROUBLE!
WHAT HAPPENED?
THE UNIVERSITY'S BLUE BOOK SUPPLIER WASN'T AMUSED WHEN I TOLD THEM I'D BE LATE WITH THEIR PAYMENT.
OUR SITUATION IS GRAVE. IF WE CAN'T RAISE ENOUGH REVENUE SOON, WE'LL HAVE TO CONVERT THIS ILLUSTRIOUS CAMPUS TO A TRUCKING SCHOOL!
IF ONLY THERE WERE SOME WAY TO EKE MORE MONEY OUT OF OUR CLASSES, LABS, ACTIVITIES...
GENTLEMEN, I BELIEVE I HAVE AN IDEA.

SOON...
...BUT ENOUGH ABOUT AYN RAND. STUDENTS, DO YOU FIND YOURSELF CRAVING REAL CAVIAR TASTE WITHOUT THE HIGH CAVIAR PRICE? THEN TRY "KRUSTYBRAND BETTER BELIEVE IT'S BELUGA-LIKE KAVIAR SUBSTITUTE!"
CLASSROOM COMMERCIALS. BRILLIANT!
...AND THE DEBATE BOYS FROM BROWN BEST LOOK OUT, 'CAUSE HERE COMES THE COOKING OIL!
HECK YEAH! KICK THEIR ACADEMIC *#@!!S!!
ROUND 6
ROUND 6
INGFIELD UNI
COME FOR THE EDUCATION, STAY FOR THE ATOMICALLY-ROASTED PORK!
GENTLEMEN, AD REVENUE IS POURING IN! CLETUS HAS SAVED THE UNIVERSITY!
MMM...AND THIS ATOMIC PORK IS TO DIE FOR! WELL, BRIGHTON? WHAT DO YOU HAVE TO SAY ABOUT THE COMMON MAN NOW?
MILK
(not grain alcohol--honest!)
CLETUS, I OWE YOU AN APOLOGY. PERHAPS, BY EXCLUDING THE TRULY STUPID, WE DENIED OURSELVES IDEAS WHICH WE COULD NEVER MUSTER FROM OUR HIGHLY ADVANCED, CULTURED BRAINS.
OH, YEAH. BRAINS IS THE BEST PART.
HA HA HEE HA HO HO
CHOKE!
WHAT DID HE JUST SAY?
THE END

EISNER AWARD WINNER!
#51
US $2.50
CAN $3.50
SIMPSONS
COMICS

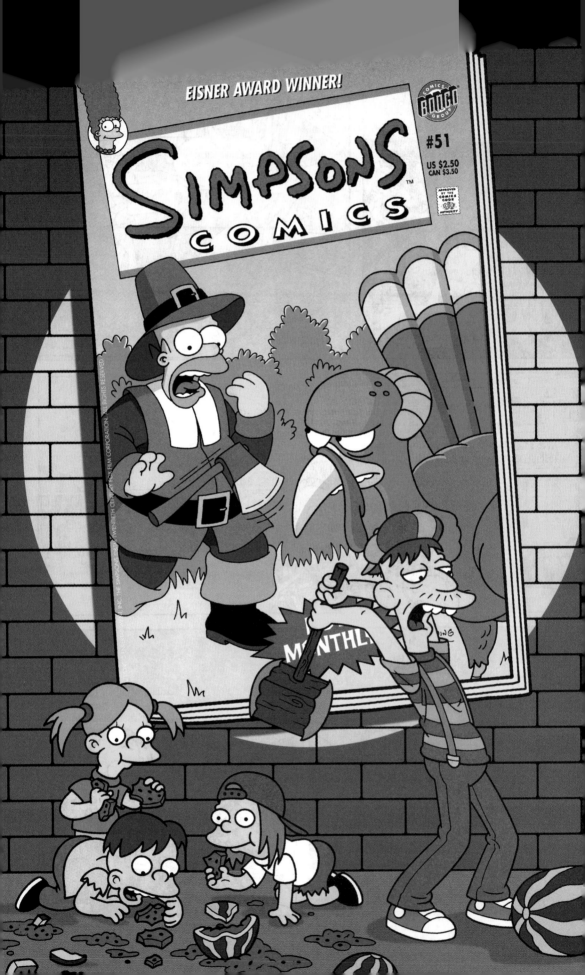

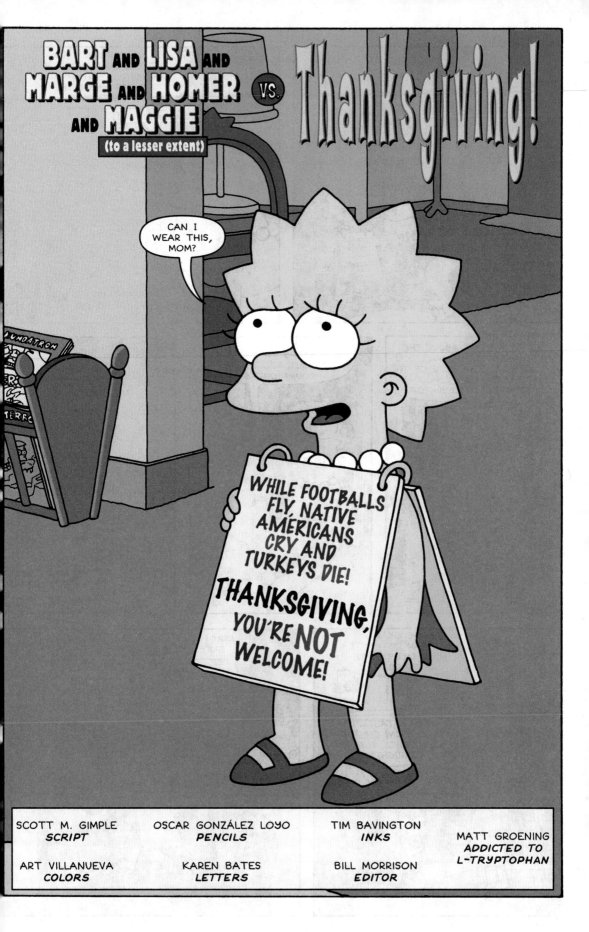

BART AND LISA AND MARGE AND HOMER AND MAGGIE (to a lesser extent) VS. Thanksgiving!

CAN I WEAR THIS, MOM?

WHILE FOOTBALLS FLY, NATIVE AMERICANS CRY AND TURKEYS DIE! THANKSGIVING, YOU'RE NOT WELCOME!

SCOTT M. GIMPLE
SCRIPT

OSCAR GONZÁLEZ LOYO
PENCILS

TIM BAVINGTON
INKS

MATT GROENING
ADDICTED TO L-TRYPTOPHAN

ART VILLANUEVA
COLORS

KAREN BATES
LETTERS

BILL MORRISON
EDITOR

LISA... NO.
BUT, MOM...
WHILE FOOTBALLS FLY, NATIVE AMERICANS CRY AND TURKEYS DIE!
THANKSGIVING, YOU'RE NOT WELCOME!
I AM NOT GOING TO LET YOU RUIN ANOTHER THANKSGIVING WITH PAINFUL TRUTHS ABOUT THE HOLIDAY!
BUT, MOM...
NO! NO PASSIONATE CONDEMNATIONS OF HYPOCRISY!
BUT, MOM! WHAT ABOUT THE FIRST AMENDMENT? CAN'T YOU SEE YOU'RE IGNORING SOME OF THE VERY FREEDOMS THE HOLIDAY SUPPOSEDLY CELEBRATES?
LISA! WHAT DID I JUST SAY?
I JUST WANT THIS TO BE A HAPPY THANKSGIVING WITHOUT POLITICS OR TOURNIQUETS.
WHILE FOOTBALLS FLY, NATIVE AMERICANS CRY AND TURKEYS DIE!
THANKSGIVING,
:SIGH: OKAY... YOU CAN DISTRIBUTE SOME LITERATURE AFTER DINNER.
WITH A TASTEFUL SLIDESHOW ON THE HORRORS OF TURKEY SLAUGHTER!
LISA! I JUST SAID--
COOL, LIS! BUT CAN YOU PUSH THE SLAUGHTERFEST TO NINE? I'M NOT GONNA BE AROUND AFTER DINNER.

WHAT? WHERE ARE YOU GOING?
TO "THE MOMENT AFTER THANKSGIVING SALE" AT THE TRY N' SAVE. "VIOLENT STICKMEN 3-D" IS COMING OUT FOR THE VIDEO GAME CONSOLE WE CURRENTLY OWN!
BART, YOU'RE STAYING HOME AFTER DINNER! TODAY IS THANKSGIVING! AND THANKSGIVING IS ABOUT FAMILY BEING TOGETHER!
...AND GENOCIDE.
WHILE FOOTBALL FLY, NATIVE AMERICANS CRY AND TURKEYS DIE!
THANKSGIVING, YOU'RE NOT WELCOME!
...WITH INCREDIBLE SAVINGS.
THAT'S IT! BOTH OF YOU, GO TO YOUR ROOMS AND DON'T COME OUT UNTIL YOU'RE THANKFUL!
WHAT A RIP...
I WANT TO GO LIVE WITH A MORE DEMOCRATIC FAMILY.
HRRRMMMMM...
MARGE, I'VE BEEN THINKING...THANKSGIVING IS ABOUT FAMILY BEING TOGETHER.
OH, HOMIE, DO YOU MEAN IT?
OF COURSE, I MEAN IT! THAT'S WHY I'VE INVITED BARNEY, LENNY, CARL, AND THOSE OTHER TWO GUYS FROM THE BAR!
YOU INVITED FIVE PEOPLE WITHOUT TELLING--
YOU'RE HOLDING A DRUMSTICK.

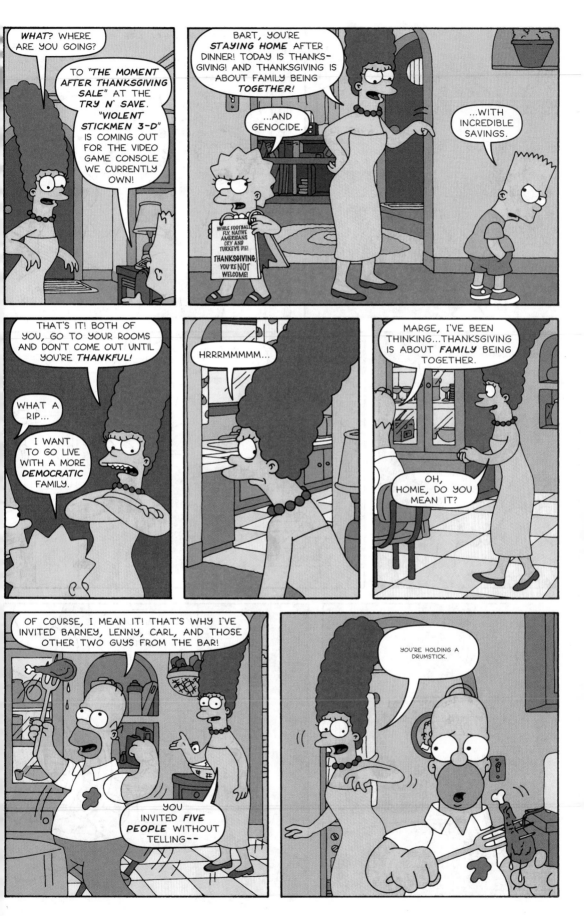

YOU TOOK THE TURKEY OUT OF THE OVEN! HOW COULD YOU EAT SIXTEEN POUNDS OF HALF-COOKED POULTRY??
IT WAS MORE LIKE A FOURTH OF THE WAY COOKED.
BUT I WRAPPED THE PIECES IN SALAMI SO THEY'D GO DOWN EASY.
HOMER, WHAT ARE WE GOING TO DO FOR THANKSGIVING DINNER? GRAMPA, SELMA, PATTY, AND MY MOTHER ARE COMING OVER!
NOT TO MENTION MY BAR FAMILY. AND MOE. DID I MENTION MOE?
URRRRRRRM...
I'M GOING TO GO GET OUT OF YOUR HAIR AND...
...DRINK.
I'LL BE AT MOE'S.
SUCK! SUCK!
OH, MAGGIE... GRAVY IS FOR GROWNUPS.

KIDS! I HAVE TO RUN TO THE **MARKET** TO FIND A TURKEY! SET THE TABLE!
AND THEN GO BACK TO YOUR ROOMS!
SLAM!
BART, I'LL PUT DOWN GLASSES AND THE CENTERPIECE, BUT I'M SORRY, I WILL **NOT** PUT DOWN PLATES!
BART?
Lisa — Left via usual Thanksgiving escape route (tree). Have fun setting table. — Bart
HRRRRRRRM.

THAT'S IT! FOR ONCE, I'M LEAVING! GIVE ME THANKSGIVING LIBERTY OR GIVE ME DEATH!
WHADAPUBUB-AAAAHH!
GAAAAAAH!
LISA! YOU SCARED THE TEETH OUTTA ME!
YOU WEAR DENTURES, GRAMPA.
I HOPE THERE'S COCONUT OIL IN YOUR SHAMPOO.
IN MY DAY, YOUNG'INS DIDN'T BARREL OUT OF DOORS DIRECTLY INTO THEIR ELDERS. THEY WOULD ALWAYS CHECK WHO WAS ON THE OTHER SIDE THROUGH A COMPLEX SYSTEM OF MIRRORS!
I'M GOING SOMEPLACE WHERE THANKSGIVING IS SEEN AS IT TRULY IS--A FESTERING SORE OF LIES AND TURKEYCIDE!
I WAS JUST HEADED OVER THERE! IF YOU WANNA GO, THE FRYBREAD'S ON YOU.
FRYBREAD?

Navajaggio
INDIAN GAMING IN THE CLASSIC ITALIAN STYLE
SEE 'K' THE ULTIMATE KRUSTY THE CLOWN ADULTS-ONLY EXPERIENCE.
OH, HOW IT'S GROWN! IT WAS JUST A TRAILER AND AN OUTHOUSE WHEN THEY OPENED IT.
WHEN WAS THAT?
LAST MONTH.
IS THAT VALET WEARING A JACKET MADE OF MARBLE?
MEANWHILE, AT THE MARKET...
HOLD IT THERE, SIMPSON. YOU WANNA GO IN, YOU HAVE TO SUIT UP.
SUIT UP?
IT'S MADNESS IN THERE. ALL CIVILITY HAS BEEN STRIPPED AWAY! IT'S A LAWLESS FRENZY OF DESPERATION THAT'S BROKEN DOWN INTO A HAIR-PULLING, GROIN-KICKING ORGY OF LOW SUPPLY, HIGH DEMAND.
WE'RE HERE TO ENSURE PEOPLE DON'T START LOOTING.
I GOTCHA THAT GROSS OF SMALL CURD COTTAGE CHEESE YOU ASKED ME TO LOOT, CHIEF.
GOOD WORK, THERE, EDDIE.
NOW WE HAVE TWO COLORS OF FLAK JACKETS, BOOBERRY AND STRAWBERRY QUIK. WHAT'S IT GONNA BE, SIMPSON?
DISCO STU SAW IT FIRST!
IT'S GOT MY FREAKIN' NAME ON IT! READ THE LABEL! IT'S KRUSTY'S KANNED KRAMBROSIA!
EXCUSE ME, DO YOU HAVE ANY TURKEYS LEFT?
NO, BUT HURRY OVER TO OUR MEAT SECTION FOR AMAZING IN-STORE SPECIALS ON DESPAIR AND HUMAN MISERY.

WHILE AT MOE'S BAR...
EERBEERBEERBEERBEER
RBEERPEANUTSBEERBEERBE
EERBEERBEERBEERBEERBEER
ERBEERBEERBEERBEERBEERB
BEERADRIENNEBARBEAUB
MOE'S
NOOOOO!
GIVIN' THANKS AT HOMER'S, GET DRUNK ELSEWHERE.
MOE, YOU'RE GIVING THANKS AT HOMER'S? HOW COULD YOU DO THIS TO ME??
SIMPSON, I'VE BEEN LOOKING ALL OVER FOR YOU!
REALLY?
WELL, NO. WE CAME HERE FIRST. YOUR FILE LISTS THIS BAR AS YOUR HOME ADDRESS.
HOMER, MR. BURNS NEEDS YOUR HELP. GET IN.
I SUPPOSE YOU WANT TO KNOW WHAT THIS IS ALL ABOUT.
EH...
IT ALL STARTED THIS MORNING...

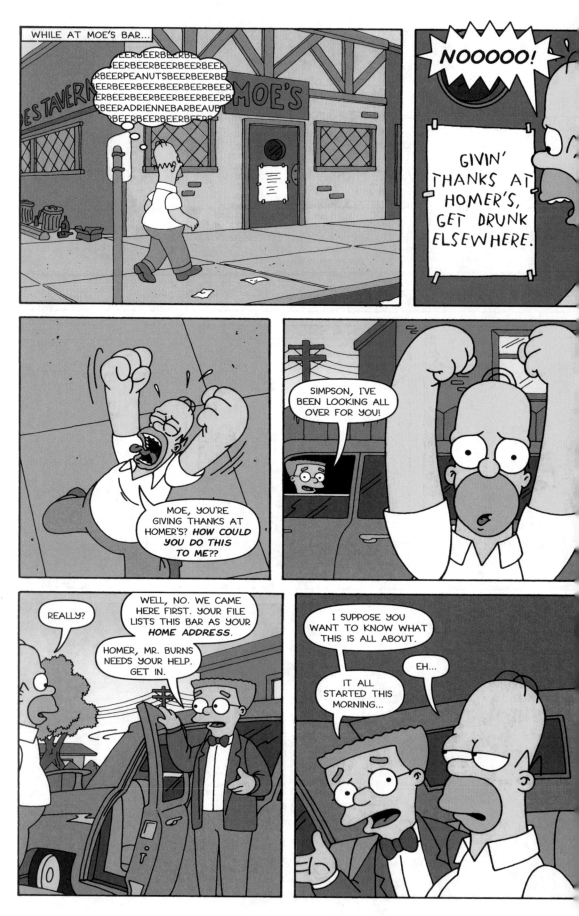

"MR. BURNS WAS STARTING HIS THANKSGIVING DAY AS HE USUALLY DOES, WITH THE *TRADITIONAL BEHEADING* OF THREE TOM TURKEYS..."
AH, THERE TRULY IS NOTHING THAT MAKES YOU FEEL MORE ALIVE THAN *KILLING,* EH SMITHERS?
IT'S JUST ONE OF THOSE *UNIVERSAL TRUTHS,* SIR.
SMITHERS, DON THE PONCHO. DEATH DRAWS NIGH FOR THE TURKEYS.
YANK!
HAH! LOOK SHARP!
WHAP!
DRAT IT! I KNEW VOLVO COULDN'T BUILD A BETTER *GUILLOTINE!*
THOUGH THESE TURKEYS LACK THE VOCAL STRUCTURE TO DO SO...MR. BURNS, THEY APPEAR TO BE *GROWLING*. I BELIEVE WE SHOULD *RUN*.

DAZED AND ANGERED BY THEIR ATTEMPTED BEHEADING, THE TURKEYS ATTACKED.
IT WAS HORRIBLE, LIKE PROFESSIONAL SQUARE DANCING. IT WAS NOTHING SHORT OF A POULTRY APOCALYPSE.
SIMPSON! WHAT ARE YOU DOING?
WHAT DOES IT LOOK LIKE? I'M GETTIN' EVEN WITH THAT KID AT THE KRUSTYBURGER WHO SHORTED ME ON PICKLES.
THIS IS NO TIME FOR MOONING! THOSE THREE TURKEYS HAVE MR. BURNS TRAPPED IN ONE OF HIS BRAN PANTRIES! I NEED YOU TO HELP ME SAVE HIM!
OKAY, OKAY. KEEP YOUR PANTS ON.
WAIT--DON'T! I HAVE A BETTER IDEA! LET'S MOON THAT KID AT THE KRUSTYBURGER!
AW, MAN...A LINE! THIS IS MY FAULT. I SHOULD'VE SNUCK OUT BEFORE DAWN.
TRY N' SAVE
HEY MAN, PSYCHED FOR THE FULLY-RENDERED RETURN OF VIOLENT STICKMEN?
SAY WHAT?
GASP!

MEANWHILE...
HEY, ABRAHAM!
ABE.
ABE.
GOOD TO SEE YOU, SIMPSON!
MY MOST SINCEREST OF SALUTATIONS, MR. SIMPSON.
DUDE, I TOLD YOU. WHO NEEDS FAKE I.D.'S WHEN YOU'VE GOT MONOCLES?
GRAMPA, HOW DO ALL THESE PEOPLE KNOW YOU?
OH, I COME BY FOR TEN OR TWELVE HOURS EVERY DAY.
TEN OR TWELVE HOURS???
WHAT DO YOU DO?
I ALTERNATE BETWEEN EATIN' FRYBREAD, PLAYING ROULETTE,
AND PASSING OUT FROM SMOKE INHALATION.
WHEN YOU CASH YOUR SOCIAL SECURITY CHECK HERE, YOU GET A FREE BOLO! HOT ZIGGETTY ZAM! THE TURQUOISE IS SHAPED LIKE A TURKEY!
A TURKEY? NOT THIS PLACE, TOO!
HEY!
HAPPY THANKSGIVING
HOW CAN YOU POSSIBLY SUPPORT A HOLIDAY THAT COMMEMORATES THE UTTER DECIMATION OF THE NATIVE AMERICAN CULTURE?
A CALLOUS CELEBRATION OF GLEEFUL REVISIONIST HISTORY, PUTTING A TURKEY AND STUFFING SMILEY FACE OVER IMPERIALISM AND VIOLENCE?
BY RELIEVING AS MANY OF YOU OF YOUR MONEY AS POSSIBLE. THANKSGIVING IS ONE OF THE BIGGEST GAMBLING DAYS OF THE YEAR.
WOULD YOU LIKE A SHRIMP COCKTAIL, LITTLE GIRL? THEY'RE ONLY A QUARTER.
WELL, THEY RELIEVED ME OF MY MONEY. LET'S GO GET US SOME CHEAPO SHRIMP COCKTAILS!

ACROSS TOWN...
OH, THANK GOODNESS!
RELEASE THE PARMESAN, HAG! I REQUIRE IT FOR MY SECRET WARS STUFFING, PART OF MY THANKSGIVING IN THE MARVEL UNIVERSE!
YES! WE HAVE TURKEYS!
LET GO OF THE CAN, TUBBO! I GOT A LOBSTER, AND I AIN'T AFRAID TO USE IT!
YES! WE HAVE TURKEYS!
WHA? NO TURKEYS! BUT THE SIGN SAID--
THE SIGN IS WRONG...
HOW COULD SUCH A BIG SIGN BE WRON-- GASP!
LISTEN CAREFULLY... I HEARD THEY HAVE A FEW BIRDS LEFT IN THE BACK...I WAS GOING THERE WHEN I GOT INTO A SKIRMISH OVER BREAD CRUMBS...I WOKE UP UNDER ALL THESE BEETS...
LET ME HELP YOU--
NO! MY FAMILY'S THANKSGIVING IS DONE FOR! YOURS YET LIVES! GO...GO NOW!
HRRRRRRMMM....
EMPLOYEES ONLY
AT STATELY BURNS MANOR...
MR. BURNS NEVER TRUSTED THE CORNISH. HE HAD THESE SUITS MADE UP AS A CONTINGENCY PLAN IN CASE THEY WERE TO SIC THEIR GAME HEN UPON THE EARTH. HE NEVER DREAMED THAT THEY WOULD ONE DAY BE USED AS A PROTECTION FROM AGITATED TURKEYS. THEY SHOULD KEEP US SAFE.
MY SUIT MAKES MY HIPS LOOK JUST AWFUL! WHY IS IT SO BULGY?
UM, MR. BURNS' SKIN IS AS THIN AS WAX PAPER. ER, HE REQUIRES A GREAT DEAL OF PADDING.

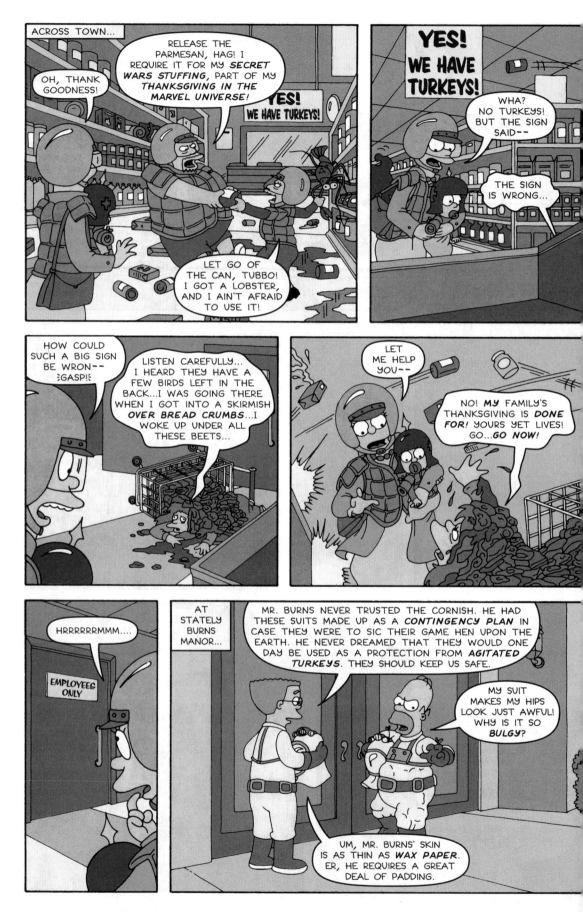

GET READY, SIMPSON. WE'RE GOING IN.
BUT *YOURS* ISN'T--
GOOD LORD! THE BIRDS HAVE CUT THE *POWER!*
I DON'T KNOW ABOUT THIS.
YOU DON'T KNOW ABOUT THIS? YOU DON'T FREAKIN' *KNOW* ABOUT THIS? WELL, *I* KNOW ABOUT THIS!
I KNOW MR. BURNS IS *IN DANGER* OF GETTING *KILLED* BY TURKEYS! I KNOW THEY'LL MAKE A *FLESHY CONFETTI* OUT OF HIM IF WE DON'T SAVE HIM! I KNOW HOW TO MAKE A *TASTY DIP* OUT OF SHORTENING AND HOT SAUCE!
AND IF *THAT* DOESN'T MAKE ME "*COOL*", THEN *CRAM IT,* SMITHERS! I'M *GOIN'* IN.
SIMPSON, IF YOU WERE MR. BURNS, I'D *KISS* YOU.
SAVE YOUR KISSIN' FOR THE TURKEYS, BOY.

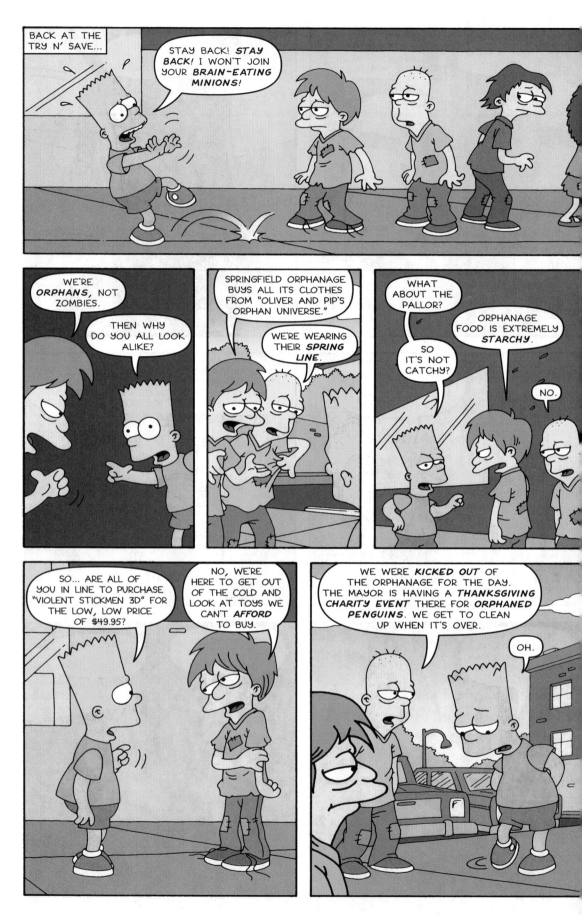

BACK AT THE TRY N' SAVE...

STAY BACK! *STAY BACK!* I WON'T JOIN YOUR *BRAIN-EATING MINIONS!*

WE'RE *ORPHANS*, NOT ZOMBIES.

THEN WHY DO YOU ALL LOOK ALIKE?

SPRINGFIELD ORPHANAGE BUYS ALL ITS CLOTHES FROM "OLIVER AND PIP'S ORPHAN UNIVERSE."

WE'RE WEARING THEIR *SPRING LINE*.

WHAT ABOUT THE PALLOR?

SO IT'S NOT CATCHY?

ORPHANAGE FOOD IS EXTREMELY *STARCHY*.

NO.

SO... ARE ALL OF YOU IN LINE TO PURCHASE "VIOLENT STICKMEN 3D" FOR THE LOW, LOW PRICE OF $49.95?

NO, WE'RE HERE TO GET OUT OF THE COLD AND LOOK AT TOYS WE CAN'T *AFFORD* TO BUY.

WE WERE *KICKED OUT* OF THE ORPHANAGE FOR THE DAY. THE MAYOR IS HAVING A *THANKSGIVING CHARITY EVENT* THERE FOR *ORPHANED PENGUINS*. WE GET TO CLEAN UP WHEN IT'S OVER.

OH.

AT THE NAVAJAGGIO...
GRAMPA, THANKS FOR TAKING ME HERE.
WHY? YOU PAID FOR THE SHRIMPS.
ALTHOUGH WE CAN NEVER TRULY MAKE GOOD ON THE TERRIBLE DEEDS WE DID TO THE NATIVE AMERICAN PEOPLE IN THE PAST, IT'S COMFORTING TO SEE WE WILL BE THEIR SUCKERS, PATSIES, AND LOSERS FOR THE FORSEEABLE FUTURE...
HOUSE GETS BLACKJACK.
OHHHHH....
...THAT THEY WILL INFLICT SUFFERING UPON US, TAKE RESOURCES FROM US,
AND THE AMERICAN PEOPLE WILL STILL LINE UP, HAPPILY AND STUPIDLY FOR THEIR BUFFETS!
IT JUST MAKES ME FEEL A LITTLE BETTER, GRAMPA.
HOW ABOUT A HUG, SWEETIE!
HEY! MY PURSE!
PITY ME! I HAVE A COMPULSION! YOU CAN HAVE MY BOLO.

INSIDE THE MARKET STORAGE ROOM...
MY GOODNESS! WHAT AM I DOING HERE? I SHOULD BE HOME CANDYING YAMS AND STIFLING MY RAGE!
REFRIGERATOR
GASP! THE REFRIGERATOR!
THE NICE LADY UNDER THE PILE OF BEETS WAS RIGHT!
KRUST-CICLES
NOW, IF I CAN TIME THIS RIGHT...
TATER TOTS
...I CAN KEEP EVERYTHING TIDY!
TATER TOTS
AND NOW, TO THE REGISTER! MY, THIS WENT WELL.
TATER TOTS
TWO MINUTES LATER...

PLEASE, MARGE, THANKSGIVING IS ALL I HAVE LEFT!
SURRENDER THE TOM!
YAAAAAAAAAH!!!!
ABANDONE EL PARVO!
SPROING!
OH, MY...
WOW. THE **CONCENTRATED FORCE** OF MY HAIR IS **INCREDIBLE**! I COULD USE IT TO SEND BOXES UP TO THE ATTIC. MY HAIR IS SO...**SPRINGY**! THANK YOU, **FINESSE**!
I'D LIKE TO BUY THIS TURKEY, PLEASE.
TURKEY? I'M AFRAID YOU'RE MISTAKEN, LADY.
LOOKS LIKE YOU GOT ONE OF "COLONEL CURIE'S **ALMOST** TURKEY." IT'S ACTUALLY A **HORMONE-RICH CHICKEN**.
GASP!
ALMOST TURKEY
YOU WANT I SHOULD WRAP IT UP FOR YA?
SIGH NO.

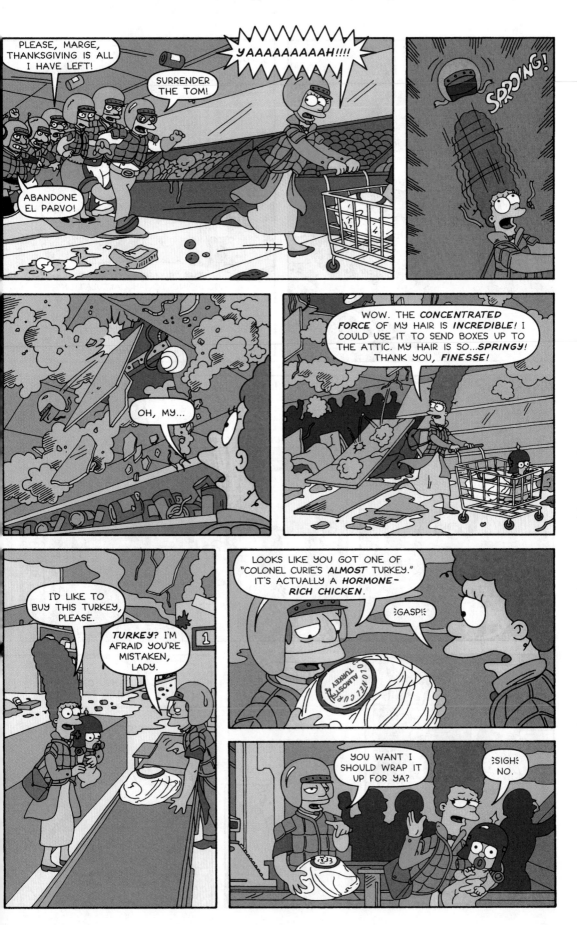

LOOK! THE DOORS ARE OPENING!
KIDS, SPRINGFIELD'S BELOVED PROFESSOR FRINK HAS AN ANNOUNCEMENT!
THAT'S, AHEM, CORRECT. ACCORDING TO MY CALCULATIONS, TAKING INTO ACCOUNT EARLY DINNERS, FOOTBALL GAMES IN DIFFERENT TIME ZONES, "FLAVIN", AND, "HOOHAY", THE DENOUEMENT OF THE CHARLIE BROWN THANKSGIVING SPECIAL, THE MOMENT AFTER THANKSGIVING IS BUT TEN SECONDS AWAY!
HOORAY!
I'M SORRY, BUT YOU KIDS LOOK A LOT LIKE PENNILESS ORPHANS. TO GET IN YOU EITHER HAVE TO BE ACCOMPANIED BY A PARENT, GUARDIAN, OR AT LEAST A COUPLE OF BUCKS.
WE JUST WANTED TO GET IN FROM THE COLD.
SORRY, STORE POLICY. HANDS'RE TIED HERE. KIDS WITH MONEY OR GUARDIANS, COME ON DOWN.
WAIT!
WHAT?
HOW MANY OF YOU ORPHANS ARE THERE?
AN ORPHANS DOZEN. TWENTY FOUR.

LISTEN, DISPERSE THESE URCHINS, KID! I HAVE CUSTOMERS TO ATTEND--
ATTEND TO US, BUDDY! I GOT FIFTY BIG ONES THAT SAY WE'RE GOIN' INSIDE TO MONOPOLIZE YOUR TRYOUT VIDEO GAMES AND FLOOR MODEL BICYCLES FOR THE NEXT TWO HOURS AT LEAST!
BUT BART, WHAT ABOUT "VIRTUAL STICKMEN"3D?
AH, I'M SURE MY BUDDY MILHOUSE WILL GET TWO COPIES. HIS PARENTS ARE DIVORCED.
DEEP IN THE BOWELS OF BURNS MANOR...
THERE ARE THE TURKEYS, SIMPSON. THEY'RE THE PRODUCT OF METICULOUS GENETIC MEDDLING THAT HAS CAUSED THEM TO BE SUPER-AGGRESSIVE. THEY'RE 99% WHITE MEAT AND THEY SWEAT BUTTER.
MMM... BUTTER SWEAT.
CLACK! GOBBLE! CLACK! GOBBLE! GOBBLE!
THIS IS IT. YOU DISTRACT THE BIRDS, I FREE MR. BURNS AND CARRY HIM TO SAFETY.
THEN YOU COME BACK AND SAVE ME BEFORE THE BIRDS MAKE ME INTO A PITIFUL PILE OF CARRION, FESTER-ING IN BURNS' RUMPUS ROOM.
LOOK AT ME, TURKEYS! I'M DISTRACTING TO A FAULT!
SORRY, SIMPSON. SO, SO SORRY...
CLIK!
WHA?
CLICK! CLICK! CLICK! CLICK!

SMITHERS, MY SUIT IS LEAKING BIRDSEED!
EER--I'M SORRY SIMPSON, WE NEEDED A FAILSAFE TARGET FOR THE TURKEYS WRATH!
SMITHERS! YOU PLAYED ME FOR A PATSY! YOU SOLD ME OUT!
EH.
MR. BURNS!
SMITHERS, YOU IDIOT! THE BRAN!
GRAINS EVERYWHERE--CAN'T ESCAPE!
A BRAN COLLAPSE! MUST SAVE EVIL BOSS AND LACKEY WHO SET ME UP!
WHAM!
HOLD ON, DEAR FRIENDS!
LOOKS LIKE WE'RE SAFE. THE BIRDS--
YEEEEEEEEK!

UH-OH, LISA. LOOKS LIKE ANOTHER ANGRY MOB OUT TO KILL YOUR FATHER. GUESS WE SHOULD START BEGGING FOR HIS LIFE.
PLEASE DON'T KILL MY BOY!
GRAMPA, THOSE PEOPLE ARE FAMILY AND FRIENDS.
WE GET HERE, NO ONE'S AROUND, THE DOOR'S BOLTED, THE WINDOWS ARE LOCKED, THE FLUE IS UP ON THE CHIMNEY...LISTEN, IF THIS IS SOME KINDA TURKEYDAY JOKE, I AIN'T LAUGHIN'!
DAD WENT TO DRINK, AND MOM WENT TO GET A TURKEY!
BRAAAAAAP!
YOU DON'T HAVE A TURKEY??
NO TURKEY? BUT I PROMISED THESE GUYS!
I GUESS WE CAN SETTLE FOR A HAM...OR A TURKEY-FLAVORED BREAK-FAST CEREAL OF SOME KIND.
I CAN'T BELIEVE I DON'T HAVE A TURKEY...
OH MY LORD!
KEEP RUNNING! I HAVE GUNS AT MY HOUSE! A MIGHTY ARSENAL OF GUNS!
GASP!
SCREEECH!

MY LORD I'VE HIT...
THREE TURKEYS!
YAAAAAY!
ALL-RIGHT!
HOORAY!
I CAN'T BELIEVE YOU SACRIFICED YOUR "VIOLENT STICKMEN" MONEY TO HELP OUT A BUNCH OF ORPHANS YOU DON'T KNOW.
SO YOU SAY I WAS TRAPPED BY THESE VERY TURKEYS WE'RE DINING ON? AND IS IT TRUE THAT THE EARTH IS NO LONGER ENSLAVED BY THE SQUID-MEN OF VENUS?
JUST SAY YES, SIMPSON. HE'S BEE THROUGH A LOT.
THIS BIRD IS KINDA DRY. COULDJA--
SORRY, GRAMPA, BUT I CAN'T BE A PARTY TO GRAVY. WHY DON'T YOU ASK MOE TO PASS....
ACTUALLY, I WAS HOPING YOU HAD MORE OF THAT COCONUT OIL SHAMPOO.

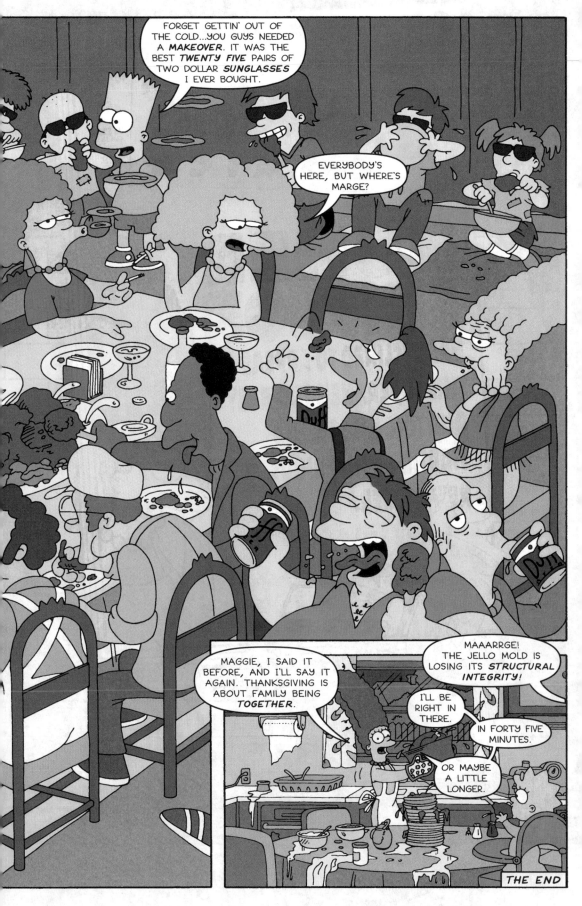

FORGET GETTIN' OUT OF THE COLD...YOU GUYS NEEDED A **MAKEOVER**. IT WAS THE BEST **TWENTY FIVE** PAIRS OF TWO DOLLAR **SUNGLASSES** I EVER BOUGHT.

EVERYBODY'S HERE, BUT WHERE'S MARGE?

MAGGIE, I SAID IT BEFORE, AND I'LL SAY IT AGAIN. THANKSGIVING IS ABOUT FAMILY BEING **TOGETHER**.

MAAARRGE! THE JELLO MOLD IS LOSING ITS **STRUCTURAL INTEGRITY**!

I'LL BE RIGHT IN THERE.

IN FORTY FIVE MINUTES.

OR MAYBE A LITTLE LONGER.

THE END

EISNER AWARD WINNER!
SIMPSONS COMICS
#53
US $2.50
CAN $3.50
HOMER SIMPSON
HAS DECLINED TO APPEAR ON THIS COVER. HE'S TOO BUSY QUITTING HIS JOB AND STARTING A HILARIOUS NEW CAREER.
HERE WE GO AGAIN!
GROENING

The Beer Boys

I'VE WAITED A *LONG TIME* FOR THIS MOMENT! I'VE FINALLY GOT YOU *RIGHT* WHERE I WANT YOU...

DOUG TUBER,
TIM MAILE,
STEVE LUCHSINGER
SCRIPT

PHIL ORTIZ
PENCILS

TIM BAVINGTON
INKS

ART VILLANUEVA
COLORS

JEANNINE BLACK
KAREN BATES
LETTERS

BILL MORRISON
EDITOR

MATT GROENING
DESIGNATED DRIVER

SPRINGFIELD NUCLEAR POWER PLANT
25 YEARS AND STILL "GLOWING" STRONG
...SAY "FISSION"!
I WANTED A PHOTO OF MY SURVIVING EMPLOYEES TO COMMEMORATE MORE THAN A QUARTER-CENTURY OF TRIUMPH OVER THOSE ANTI-POISON HYSTERIA-MONGERS. AS A TOKEN OF MY GRATITUDE, YOU'LL ALL RECEIVE A WALLET-SIZED PRINT AND FIVE "BURNS BUCKS," REDEEMABLE AT THE COMPANY GIFT SHOP.
CONGRATULATIONS, FACELESS COG.
HEY, THANKS! I'M GONNA GET A TUBE OF NEW CAR SMELL!
FELICITATIONS, INTERCHANGEABLE FLOTSAM.
MAYNARD EZEKIEL Mc CHIMPY, WELL DONE!
I DON'T BELIEVE IT! HE SKIPPED RIGHT OVER ME FOR A MONKEY!
HEE, HEE, MONKEYS. THEY CAN RIDE TRICYCLES, THEY'VE BEEN ASTRONAUTS, AND THEY CAN GIVE PEOPLE THE FINGER!

SOON, AT THE KWIK-E-MART...
I'M FEELING LOW, APU. GIVE ME A PEPPERONI-FLAVORED SKINNY GINNY, PEPPERONI-FLAVORED SHEEP RINDS, SOME PEPPERONI NUGGETS, AND A SLICE OF PLAIN CHEESE PIZZA.
HELP KRUSTY'S KIDS FIGHT GIGANTISM BIGGER ISN'T ALWAYS BETTER!
WHILE YOU'RE AT IT, HELP KRUSTY!
DON'T EXPECT ANY FREE PENNIES!
I AM AFRAID I CANNOT HONOR THAT REQUEST.
WE RESERVE THE RIGHT TO REFUSE SERVICE TO ANYONE.
BUT... YOU...ME... HUNGRY.
IF WE DO NOT EXERCISE OUR RIGHTS, WE LOSE THEM. SO, I PERIODICALLY REFUSE TO SERVE RIFF-RAFF.
I'M NOT RIFF-RAFF.
RIFF-RAFF, SAD-SACK, GOOSE EGG-- IT IS A MATTER OF SEMANTICS.
BURY HIM
EVERYDAY FUNERALS FOR EVERYDAY FOLK
RASSA-FRACKIN' RIFF-RAFF...RASSA-FRACKIN' SAD-SACK... I'M HOMER SIMPSON! I HAVE DIGNITY!
SPLOOSH!
D' GURGLE OH!
HEY, THAT WAS MY TRASH WATER 'N ROADKILL PARTS! IT WAS S'POSED TO GO IN THE GUTTER! YOU DONE WENT 'N RUIN'D IT!

...AND THEN A HILLBILLY THREW TRASH WATER ON ME LIKE I WASN'T EVEN THERE. I'M A NOBODY, MARGE!
NOW, HOMER--
I'VE GOT A NOWHERE JOB, AND A NOWHERE LIFE, AND A NOWHERE FAMILY.
PLUS YOU SMELL LIKE THE TIME MY PET TURTLE CRAWLED INTO THE HEATING DUCT AND DIED.
I DON'T HAPPEN TO THINK YOUR CHILDREN AND YOUR WIFE ARE NOWHERE.
NOW, NOW, MARGE, IT'S SWEET OF YOU TO TRY TO CHEER ME UP, BUT YOU ARE NOWHERE. EACH AND EVERY ONE OF YOU.
NOW, IF YOU'LL EXCUSE ME, I'M GOING TO MOE'S, WHERE I GET SOME RESPECT, AND WHERE PEOPLE ANSWER WHEN I SPEAK TO THEM...
GIMME A DUFF, MOE.

MOE?
FLOP!
WHAM!
YEAH, MOE'S BEEN DOIN' THAT ALL NIGHT. I THINK HE'S REALLY SICK.
THANK GOODNESS. I THOUGHT HE WAS IGNORING ME.
NOT...SICK. PERFECTLY... FINE.
FEEL...SWELL. JUST HAVE TO...GO IN HERE A MINUTE...
El Barto

MEN
766-1111
JOE
711-8811
Duff
CIGARET
MEN
EEAAAGGGGHHHHH!
OH-MY-SWEET-MERCIFUL-LORD!
766-1111
JOE
711-8811
AGGGHH! IT BURNS! IT BURNS! I CAN'T BELIEVE THE AGONY!
I CAN'T STAND IT! IT'S TERRIBLE, I TELLS YA! IT'S TERRIBLE!
HEH, HEH. MOE MUST'VE SEEN A SPIDER. 'FRAIDY-CAT.
IF I MAY OFFER ANOTHER OPINION, THAT'S NOT THE SCREAM OF A 'FRAIDY-CAT. NO, THAT'S A MAN SUFFERING FROM HIDEOUSLY PAINFUL GALLSTONES. PROBABLY PASSED ONE THE SIZE OF A WAFFLE IRON. AH, HEE, HEE, HEE!
MOE, I'M EXTREMELY CONCERNED.
I NEVER GOT MY BEER. AND THE DOC SAYS YOU'RE REALLY SICK.
766-1111
JOE
711-8811
SO I'M SICK. BIG DEAL. FDR HAD POLIO, AND HE WAS PRESIDENT FOR 12 YEARS. IF I GET AN OPERATION, I'LL HAVE TO SHUT THIS PLACE DOWN FOR A WEEK!

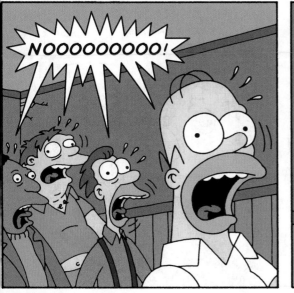

NOOOOOOOOOO!

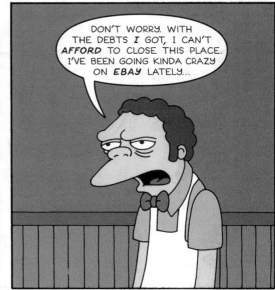

DON'T WORRY. WITH THE DEBTS *I* GOT, I CAN'T *AFFORD* TO CLOSE THIS PLACE. I'VE BEEN GOING KINDA CRAZY ON *EBAY* LATELY...

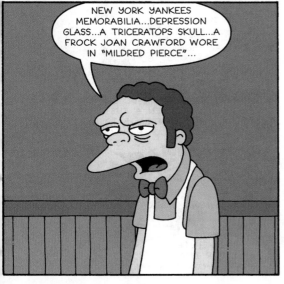

NEW YORK YANKEES MEMORABILIA...DEPRESSION GLASS...A TRICERATOPS SKULL...A FROCK JOAN CRAWFORD WORE IN "MILDRED PIERCE"...

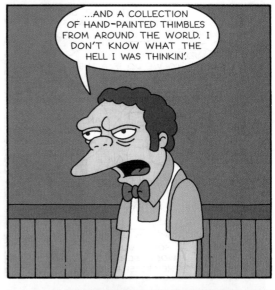

...AND A COLLECTION OF HAND-PAINTED THIMBLES FROM AROUND THE WORLD. I DON'T KNOW WHAT THE HELL I WAS THINKIN'.

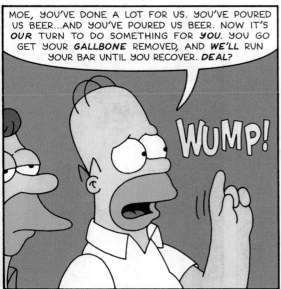

MOE, YOU'VE DONE A LOT FOR US. YOU'VE POURED US BEER...AND YOU'VE POURED US BEER. NOW IT'S *OUR* TURN TO DO SOMETHING FOR *YOU*. YOU GO GET YOUR *GALLBONE* REMOVED, AND *WE'LL* RUN YOUR BAR UNTIL YOU RECOVER. *DEAL*?

WUMP!

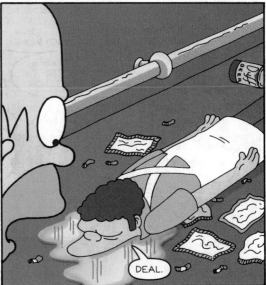

DEAL.

SOON...
YOU'RE GOING TO RUN A BAR? I'M NOT SURE I WANT YOU DOING THAT.
ALL RIGHT, THAT DOES IT...
SEE, BART? THIS IS GOOD PRACTICE FOR TOSSING OUT ORNERY DRUNKS.
OUT YOU GO, BOOZEHOUND!
ALL RIGHT, ALL RIGHT! LET ME GO!
MAYBE IT'S A GOOD THING THAT YOU'RE HELPING MOE. HELPING OUR FRIENDS IS GOOD, CHRISTIAN CHARITY.
YES, IT IS...QUICK, BART, WHAT DO WE DO IF A LUSH STIFFS US ON A CHECK?
CHASE HIM INTO THE ALLEY AND BEAT HIM IN THE KIDNEYS WITH A SOCK FULL OF QUARTERS.
NO, A SOCK FULL OF WOOD SCREWS. THEY'RE SHARPER.
'KAY, HOMEY. WHAT'S IN A COSMOPOLITAN?
WE SERVE BEER! YOU WANT SOME FANCY, BALLERINA DRINK, GO BACK TO FRANCE.
GOOD. AND WHAT DO YOU SAY WHEN A CUSTOMER'S WIFE CALLS, TRYING TO FIND THE HENPECKED SOUSE?
"HE'S NOT HERE. HE'S OUT BUYING YOU CHOCOLATES AND A BIG THING OF JEWELRY."
HEH-HEH, SHE'LL FALL FOR THAT, THE BONBON CHOMPING HARPY.
LOOK, DAD, I'VE DESIGNED COCKTAIL NAPKINS LISTING EACH OF THE TEN COMMANDMENTS. THEY FEATURE MIDDLE-AGED BUSINESSMEN OUT ON THE TOWN WITH SUSPICIOUSLY LARGE-BOSOMED WOMEN.
GOOD. THEY'LL REMEMBER THE IMAGE LONG AFTER THE POINTLESS MORAL LESSON.
THOU SHALT NOT COVET THY NEIGHBOR'S WIFE
AND NOW...

...THE BAR IS OPEN.
OLIVE, CHERRY, OLIVE, CHERRY. GREEN, RED, GREEN, RED. IT'S LIKE EATING CHRISTMAS.
THIS IS LIKE BEING A KID IN A CANDY STORE! EXCEPT THE **CANDY** GIVES YOU A **FALSE** SENSE OF WELL-BEING, AND EVENTUALLY **TURNS** YOUR LIVER INTO A LUMP OF **ASPHALT**.
RING!
HEL-LOOO!
GET BARNEY AWAY FROM THE TAPS, HOMER. AND QUIT EATING THE GARNISHES.
UM...I HAVE NO IDEA WHAT YOU'RE TALKING ABOUT, MOE. HOW ARE THINGS AT THE HOSPITAL?
I THINK MY H.M.O. IS DOIN' THIS ON THE **CHEAP**. I GO UNDER THE KNIFE RIGHT AFTER A DECLAWING AND A NEUTERING. MAN, I HOPE THEY DON'T GET THE CHARTS **MIXED UP**.
OKAY, MR. SZYSLAK, TIME TO FEEL YOUR NOSE, BOY. I HOPE YOU HAVEN'T BEEN **LICKING** YOURSELF AGAIN.
GOTTA GO, HOMER. GET BARNEY AWAY FROM THE URINAL CAKES.
TOO LATE.
CLICK!
HEY, THIS **COOKIE** TASTES LIKE A **PINE TREE**!
SET ME UP, BOYS. EDNA NEEDS HER EYE-OPENER.

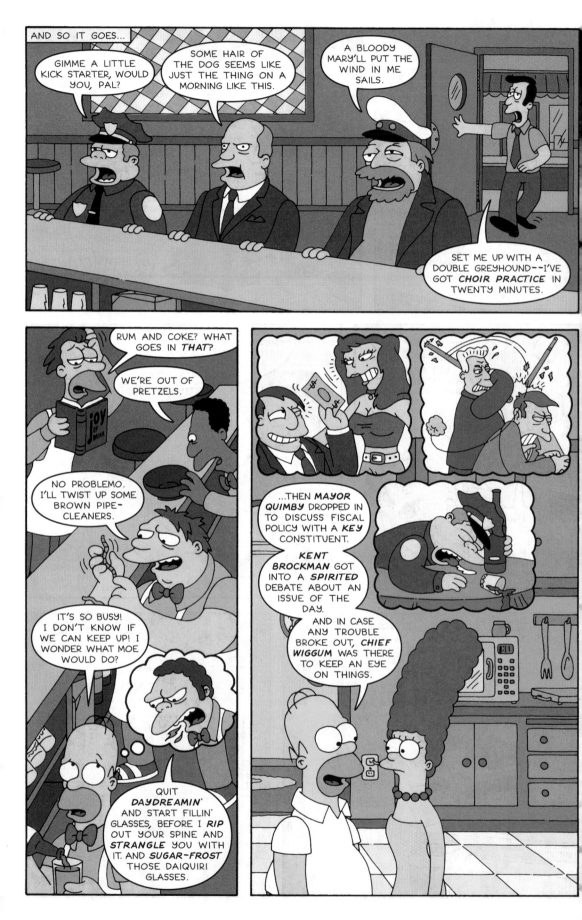

AND SO IT GOES...

GIMME A LITTLE KICK STARTER, WOULD YOU, PAL?

SOME HAIR OF THE DOG SEEMS LIKE JUST THE THING ON A MORNING LIKE THIS.

A BLOODY MARY'LL PUT THE WIND IN ME SAILS.

SET ME UP WITH A DOUBLE GREYHOUND--I'VE GOT *CHOIR PRACTICE* IN TWENTY MINUTES.

RUM AND COKE? WHAT GOES IN *THAT*?

WE'RE OUT OF PRETZELS.

NO PROBLEMO. I'LL TWIST UP SOME BROWN PIPE-CLEANERS.

IT'S SO BUSY! I DON'T KNOW IF WE CAN KEEP UP! I WONDER WHAT MOE WOULD DO?

QUIT *DAYDREAMIN'* AND START FILLIN' GLASSES, BEFORE I *RIP* OUT YOUR SPINE AND *STRANGLE* YOU WITH IT. AND *SUGAR-FROST* THOSE DAIQUIRI GLASSES.

...THEN *MAYOR QUIMBY* DROPPED IN TO DISCUSS FISCAL POLICY WITH A *KEY* CONSTITUENT.

KENT BROCKMAN GOT INTO A *SPIRITED* DEBATE ABOUT AN ISSUE OF THE DAY.

AND IN CASE ANY TROUBLE BROKE OUT, *CHIEF WIGGUM* WAS THERE TO KEEP AN EYE ON THINGS.

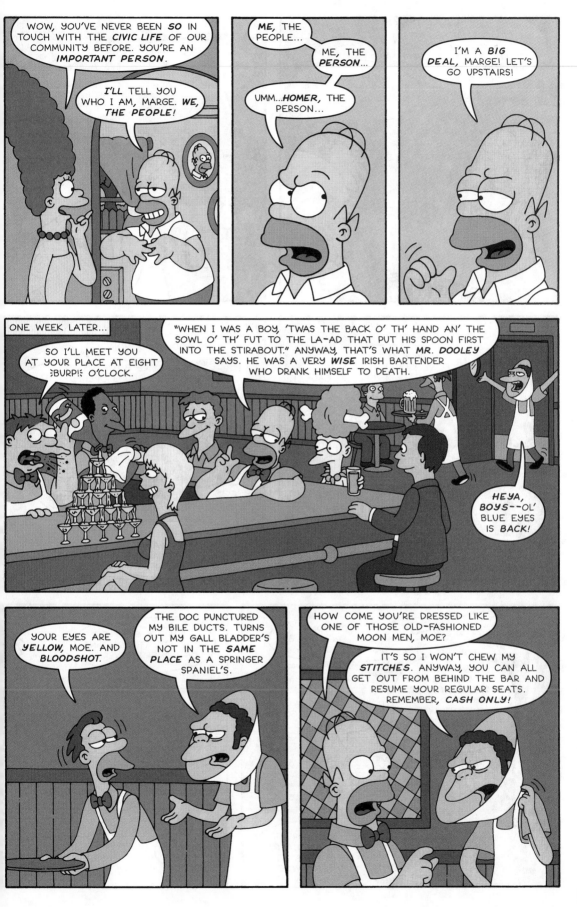

WOW, YOU'VE NEVER BEEN *SO* IN TOUCH WITH THE *CIVIC LIFE* OF OUR COMMUNITY BEFORE. YOU'RE AN *IMPORTANT PERSON*.

I'LL TELL YOU WHO I AM, MARGE. *WE, THE PEOPLE!*

ME, THE PEOPLE...

ME, THE *PERSON*...

UMM...*HOMER,* THE PERSON...

I'M A *BIG DEAL,* MARGE! LET'S GO UPSTAIRS!

ONE WEEK LATER...

SO I'LL MEET YOU AT YOUR PLACE AT EIGHT ≿BURP!≾ O'CLOCK.

"WHEN I WAS A BOY, 'TWAS THE BACK O' TH' HAND AN' THE SOWL O' TH' FUT TO THE LA-AD THAT PUT HIS SPOON FIRST INTO THE STIRABOUT." ANYWAY, THAT'S WHAT *MR. DOOLEY* SAYS. HE WAS A VERY *WISE* IRISH BARTENDER WHO DRANK HIMSELF TO DEATH.

HEYA, BOYS--OL' BLUE EYES IS *BACK!*

YOUR EYES ARE *YELLOW,* MOE. AND *BLOODSHOT.*

THE DOC PUNCTURED MY BILE DUCTS. TURNS OUT MY GALL BLADDER'S NOT IN THE *SAME PLACE* AS A SPRINGER SPANIEL'S.

HOW COME YOU'RE DRESSED LIKE ONE OF THOSE OLD-FASHIONED MOON MEN, MOE?

IT'S SO I WON'T CHEW MY *STITCHES*. ANYWAY, YOU CAN ALL GET OUT FROM BEHIND THE BAR AND RESUME YOUR REGULAR SEATS. REMEMBER, *CASH ONLY!*

GEE, MOE, MAYBE WE COULD KEEP HELPING YOU OUT. YOU KNOW, ALL PITCHING IN **TOGETHER,** ONE FOR ALL AND ALL FOR ONE...
I DON'T NEED HELP, I NEED **CUSTOMERS**. NOW BUY SOME BEER AND SHUT UP.
BEER NUTS
30 SECONDS LATER...
REMEMBER WHEN **WE** USED TO BE THE ONES PULLING THE BEER TAP, FELLAS?
THOSE WERE THE BEST DAYS OF MY LIFE.
MAYBE THOSE DAYS DON'T HAVE TO END. I'VE GOT AN IDEA...
I'M **WAY AHEAD** OF YOU. WE KIDNAP MOE, KEEP HIM IN A TINY, UNDERGROUND CAGE, FEEDING HIM TINY PELLETS OF VEGETABLE PROTEIN....
...JUST ENOUGH TO KEEP HIM **ALIVE,** AND **WE** CONTINUE RUNNING HIS BAR!
ACTUALLY, I WAS THINKING OF OPENING OUR **OWN** BAR, BUT YOUR IDEA'S GOOD TOO, HOMER.
THEY'RE **BOTH** STUPID IDEAS. IF YOU GUYS OPENED A BAR, YOU'D LOSE YOUR SHIRTS. AND AS FOR **KIDNAPPING** ME, THE CAGE HASN'T BEEN **BUILT** THAT CAN HOLD **SZYSLAK**...
...AS I THINK BOTH THE VIETCONG **AND** THE CANADIAN CUSTOMS SERVICE CAN TESTIFY.
WE'LL NEED **MONEY** TO OPEN A BAR.
I'VE GOT SOME CASH LEFT FROM MY BIG "FAMILY FEUD" WIN.
I CAN INVEST MY **DISABILITY SETTLEMENT**. THEY ALWAYS SAID EATING LEAD PAINT WAS A **BAD THING,** BUT **I** TURNED IT INTO A **POSITIVE**.
LISA'S COLLEGE FUND IS JUST SITTING THERE DOING NOTHING. **NOTHING!** WELL, **THAT'S** GONNA CHANGE.
MY MARRIAGE TO **MARTHA RAE** LEFT ME A LITTLE **INHERITANCE** TO PLAY WITH.
THEN IT'S **SETTLED**. HERE'S TO THE OPENING OF HOMER'S TAVERN.
CARL'S HIDEAWAY.
LENNY'S BAR.
LE CAFE SOPHISTICATE DE BARNEY.

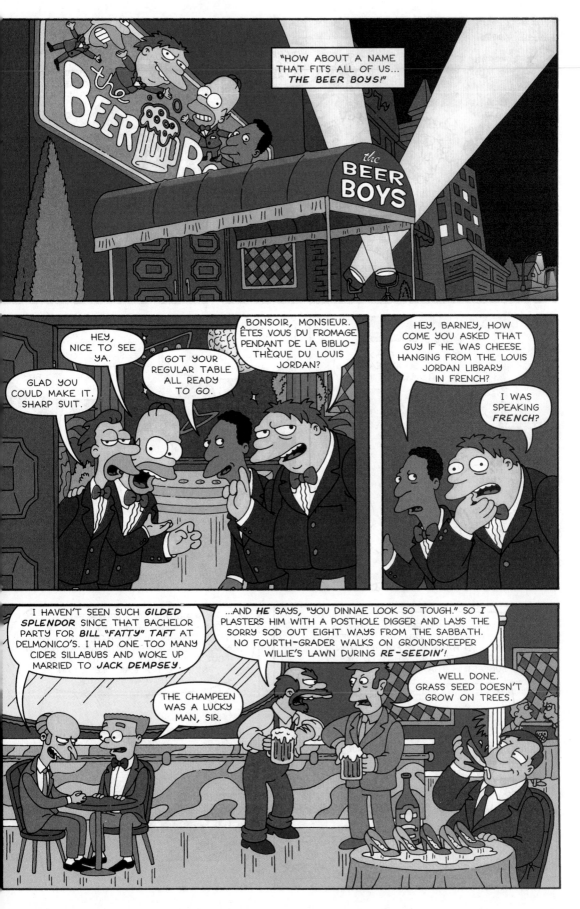

"HOW ABOUT A NAME THAT FITS ALL OF US... *THE BEER BOYS!*"

HEY, NICE TO SEE YA.

GLAD YOU COULD MAKE IT. SHARP SUIT.

GOT YOUR REGULAR TABLE ALL READY TO GO.

BONSOIR, MONSIEUR. ÊTES VOUS DU FROMAGE PENDANT DE LA BIBLIO- THÈQUE DU LOUIS JORDAN?

HEY, BARNEY, HOW COME YOU ASKED THAT GUY IF HE WAS CHEESE HANGING FROM THE LOUIS JORDAN LIBRARY IN FRENCH?

I WAS SPEAKING *FRENCH?*

I HAVEN'T SEEN SUCH *GILDED SPLENDOR* SINCE THAT BACHELOR PARTY FOR *BILL "FATTY" TAFT* AT DELMONICO'S. I HAD ONE TOO MANY CIDER SILLABUBS AND WOKE UP MARRIED TO *JACK DEMPSEY.*

THE CHAMPEEN WAS A LUCKY MAN, SIR.

...AND *HE* SAYS, "YOU DINNAE LOOK SO TOUGH." SO *I* PLASTERS HIM WITH A POSTHOLE DIGGER AND LAYS THE SORRY SOD OUT EIGHT WAYS FROM THE SABBATH. NO FOURTH-GRADER WALKS ON GROUNDSKEEPER WILLIE'S LAWN DURING *RE-SEEDIN'!*

WELL DONE. GRASS SEED DOESN'T GROW ON TREES.

YOU'RE IN, YOU'RE OUT, YOU'RE IN.
SPLENDID. I'VE GAINED ENTRANCE TO THE SANCTUM.
WRONG! I JUST CALLED YOU "URINE." YOU'RE OUT. HEH-HEH.
HEY, THERE, LITTLE BART. I NEED TO SPEAK TO YOUR DADDY.
LISTEN, YOU RUMMY, THIS IS A CLASSY JERNT. WHY SHOULD I LET YOU IN?
I'LL GIVE YOU FOUR GOOD REASONS TO LET ME IN.
HEY, HOMER, NICE PLACE YOU GOT HERE. NOBODY'S PASSED OUT IN THEIR OWN SICK OR NOTHIN'.
WELL, WELL, IF IT ISN'T MOE, THE GUY WHO SAID I'D LOSE MY SHIRT. I STILL HAVE MY SHIRT, MOE, AND I'M GOING TO BUY MORE SHIRTS.
I'M GOING TO BUY A SHIRT MADE OF SOLID GOLD. AND GOLD MOTH BALLS, TO KEEP IT NICE.
AH, IT'S GREAT TO SEE YOU DOING SO WELL, HOMER. IT'S OBVIOUS YOU'VE NEVER BEEN SO HAPPY OR FULFILLED IN YOUR ENTIRE LIFE. AND WHAT I'D LIKE TO SUGGEST IS THAT YOU QUIT IT.
OH, I GET IT. RUNNING SCARED, EH?
SCARED? I AIN'T NEVER BEEN SCARED IN MY LIFE. EXCEPT BY THOSE STICK PEOPLE IN "BLAIR WITCH," AND I WAS GONNA THROW THOSE PANTS AWAY, ANYHOW. BUT IF YOU DON'T WANT TO QUIT ALL NICE AND PEACEFUL-LIKE, I CAN PLAY IT THAT WAY, TOO.

THE BEER BOYS ARE IN IT FOR THE LONG HAUL. THE FOUR OF US ARE UNITED. LIKE PETER, PAUL, AND MARY... AND PETER AGAIN.
COME BACK TO MY PLACE, BARNEY. I'LL GIVE YOU TWO-FOR-ONE BEERS IF YOU QUIT HERE.
I'M OUTTA HERE!
ZIP!
A FEW NIGHTS LATER...
I NEVER THOUGHT ABOUT THIS BEFORE. WHEN YOU OWN A BAR, THERE'S REALLY NO PLACE TO GO AFTER WORK.
PSSST...YOU GUYS...
AAGGGGH!
YAAAAAAAAGGH!
WAAAAAAAGGHHH!
AW, THESE WERE NEW PANTS, TOO. ANYWAY, I THOUGHT YOU GUYS SHOULD KNOW, I'VE BEEN TALKING TO FAT TONY ABOUT YOU TWO. HE GAVE ME SOME PROMOTIONAL MATERIALS.
SO YOU WANT "THAT LITTLE MATTER" TAKEN CARE OF
$99.95
$199.95
$499.95
$999.95
ALL FIVE SERVICES, $1599.95...
ASK ABOUT OUR SENIORS DISCOUNT

HERE'S THE THING. I CAN'T EVEN AFFORD TO HAVE YOUR LEGS BUSTED. ON TOP OF THE FEE, I GOTTA PAY SOCIAL SECURITY, WORKMAN'S COMP, AND ON AND ON.
SO I'M THINKIN', I PAY YOU GUYS **HALF** OF WHAT IT'D COST TO SMASH YOUR DRINKIN' HANDS, AND YOU **QUIT** THE BEER BOYS AND COME BACK TO MY PLACE.
GREAT TO BE BACK, MOE.
YEAH. I DON'T KNOW WHY WE EVER WANTED TO BE PART OF THE BEER BOYS IN THE FIRST PLACE.
BACK AT "THE BEER BOYS"...
¡MIRA! ¡YO SOY EN FUEGO!
LISTEN, SWEETIE, I'LL GIVE YOU AN EXTRA FIVE HUNDRED BUCKS, IF YOU LET ME EAT MY BUFFALO WINGS OFF THE SMALL OF YOUR BACK.
HRRMM...
DIS PLACE IS DA TOPS. LIKE A **FIRST-RATE** DISCO IN LONDON, ONLY WITHOUT ALL DA KUWAITIS.
GET A LOAD OF **ME**! I'M GIVIN' OUT **WINGS**!
HOMER, KRUSTY JUST OFFERED ME **FIVE HUNDRED DOLLARS** TO LET HIM EAT AN APPETIZER OFF MY **BACKSIDE**!
HOPE YOU HELD OUT FOR A **GRAND**, MARGE. HE'S **LOUSY** WITH SCRATCH.

I DON'T LIKE WHAT'S GOING ON HERE. LISA'S PLAYING TORCH SONGS FOR SAD DRUNKS. BART'S TAKING BRIBES FROM SCENESTERS WHO WANT A GOOD TABLE. AND *I'VE* BEEN PROPOSITIONED BY A *CLOWN*!
THAT'S JUST THE *BEGINNING!* SOON I'M GOING TO BE THE ONLY BAR IN TOWN. LOOK AT THESE FLYERS--I'M GOING TO GIVE AWAY FREE BEER UNTIL *EVERYBODY* COMES HERE, AND MOE IS *OUT OF BUSINESS!*
WELL, I THINK THIS HAS GONE FAR ENOUGH. MAYBE IT'S TIME FOR YOU TO STOP.
AND WITH LENNY, CARL AND BARNEY OUT OF THE PICTURE, I'M JUST GETTING STARTED! I'M FINALLY *SOMEBODY*, MARGE, AND I WON'T STOP UNTIL I'M THE BIGGEST SOMEBODY IN THE WHOLE, WONDERFUL WORLD OF ALCOHOL! I'LL BE... *THE BRANDYMAN!*
♪ WHO CAN TAKE ♪ SOME VODKA, SHAKE IT UP WITH ICE, POUR IT DOWN YOUR ♪ GULLET TILL THE WORLD SEEMS ♪ REALLY NICE? THE BRANDYMAN. THE BRANDYMAN CAN IF ♪ YOU'RE OVER 21... ♪
♪ ...OR JUST *16* ♪ IN *AMSTERDAM!*
I'M NOT SURE I LIKE YOU AS A *SOMEBODY*. I'M GOING TO GO HOME AND WAIT UNTIL YOU'RE A *NOBODY* AGAIN.
DON'T WAIT UP, MARGE. I'M PUTTING THESE FLYERS UP AFTER WORK. HEH, HEH. I'M EVEN GONNA PLASTER 'EM ALL OVER *MOE'S!*

LATER...
OKAY, THESE ARE UP ALL OVER TOWN.
BEER BOYS!
FREE BEER! BEER BOYS!
FREE BEER! BEER BOYS!
DRINK UP, BOYS--MOE'S IS HISTORY.
FREE BEER! BEER BOYS!
FREE BEER!
CAN'T YOU KEEP THE PLACE OPEN A LITTLE WHILE LONGER, MOE?
I COULD HANG ON A FEW MORE WEEKS, LETTING KIDS BUY ADULT NOVELTIES FROM THE MACHINE IN THE TOILET, BUT GOOD TIMES CAN'T GO ON FOREVER--IT'S TIME TO CLOSE DOWN AND JUST TREASURE OUR GOLDEN MEMORIES OF MOE'S.
GOLDEN MEMORIES...
HEY, HOMER, YOUR WIFE JUST HAD A BOY.
OH, I S'POSE I SHOULD GET TO THE HOSPITAL.
RELAX, YOU GOT TIME FOR ONE MORE.
HEY, A QUARTER! TALK ABOUT YOUR BLIND LUCK!

HEY, HOMER-- YOUR WIFE JUST HAD A GIRL.
THAT'S NICE. I SHOULD STOP BY THE HOSPITAL SOMETIME.
IT'S NOT LIKE THE BABY'S GOING ANYWHERE. HAVE ANOTHER.
HOT TAMALE
GOAT CHEESE TARTLET
LIMP NOODLE
COLD FISH
OOH, "LIMP NOODLE."
WAY TO GO, HOMER. YOU JUST SET THE RECORD FOR THIS PLACE!
MARGE HAD ANOTHER GIRL, HOMER.
HIT ME AGAIN, MOE.
MOTHER TERESA... THINKSH SHE'SH A BIG DEAL... I'LL SHOW HER!
AW, LOOK AT THE LITTLE FELLA. ALL TUCKERED OUT.
I GOT A TERRIBLE INFECTION FROM THAT DIRTY BAR TOWEL. MOE GAVE ME HIS VERY OWN OINTMENT TO SMEAR ON IT, AND THIS IS HOW I REPAY HIM.
NO POINT KEEPING THE PLACE OPEN WITHOUT HOMER, ANYWAY. MOE'S WITH-OUT HOMER IS LIKE A PIG WITHOUT STINK.

MOE, YOUR PIG STINK IS BACK!
BUT WHAT ABOUT YOUR PLACE?
THIS PLACE IS WHERE I BELONG. THIS IS WHERE MY CHILDREN WERE BORN. I DON'T NEED MY BAR TO BE A SOMEBODY--
I'LL ALWAYS BE SOMEBODY RIGHT HERE!
NOW I NEED TO FIGURE OUT WHAT TO DO WITH MY PLACE.
HERE, MAYBE THIS'LL HELP.
LET'S SEE, I COULD COLLECT FIRE INSURANCE. OR I COULD USE THE SPACE IN A WAY THAT WILL BENEFIT MANKIND...
SO, YOU WANT TO COLLECT ON YOUR INSURANCE
THE BISTRO
AND AT THE CLUBHOUSE TURN IT'S DANCIN' MIRANDA, DRIVEN BY JOCKO, BUT HE-E-E-RE COMES SEXY SADIE, DRIVEN BY MR. JIG-JIG! WHAT A MAGILLAH!

I'VE GOT TO SEE A MAN ABOUT AN OSTRICH, BUT SAVE MY BARSTOOL FOR ME. AS GOD IS MY WITNESS, I'LL NEVER LEAVE MOE'S AGAIN!
IT WORKED LIKE A CHARM, MARGE. WE JUST HAD TO REMIND HIM HOW MUCH HE LOVES THIS PLACE, AND HE CAME CRAWLING BACK.
I'M NOT COMPLETELY HAPPY THAT HE'LL BE SPENDING ALL HIS TIME HERE AGAIN, BUT AT LEAST HE'LL BE BACK TO HIS OLD SELF.
JUST PROMISE ME THAT YOU'LL SEND HIM HOME OCCASIONALLY.
'S TAVERN
MOE'S
I WILL, MARGE. I WILL.
THE END

YOUR PRAYERS HAVE BEEN FLANSWERED!
APPROVED BY A HIGHER AUTHORITY
IT'S...
NED FLANDERS
HOMER SIMPSON'S FAVORITE NEIGHBOR!
BONGO COMICS GROUP
#1
US $2.50
CAN $3.50
REMEMBER, COMICS ROT YOUR BRAIN!
GROENING
J.HO

HI-DILLY-HO, NEIGHBORINOS!
WELCOME TO THE FIRST INSTALLMENT OF MY BRAND SPANKIN' NEW CABLE ACCESS TV SHOW, WHERE WE VISIT THE HISTORIC LOCALES OF GOOD, OLD SPRINGFIELD.
Around Town with Ned Flanders
Bless this Mess
YOU KNOW, IT WASN'T LONG AFTER OUR TOWN WAS DISCOVERED BY JEBEDIAH SPRINGFIELD--OL' HEATHEN THOUGH HE WAS--THAT THE FIRST CHURCH WAS BUILT USING LOGS, MUD AND THE NATIVE'S TEEPEES.
WELL, SIR, OUR HOUSES OF WORSHIP HAVE COME A LONG WAY SINCE THEN, FROM "PASTOR PAT'S REVIVAL HALL FOR THUMPIN' AND HOLY ROLLIN'" IN THE '30'S, TO REVEREND LOVEJOY'S MODERN GLASS SANCTUARY OF TODAY.
THESE ARE JUST A FEW OF THE EXCI-DIDDILY-ITING LOCATIONS WE'LL BE EXAMINING IN FULL DETAIL ON TODAY'S SHOW!
WITH THE HELP OF MY TWO, TRUE-BLUE, CREW-BUDDIES: ROD, BEHIND THE CAMERA, AND TODD ON SOUND...
WE'LL HAVE A FAN-DIDDILY-TASTIC TIME AS WE SEE THE SIGHTS OF SPRINGFIELD!
YOU BOYS HAVE FUN. I PACKED SANDWICHES!
SO, SHALL WE FIRE UP THE OL' FLANDERS-MOBILE?
YOU BET YOUR BIPPY! THE WONDERFUL WORLD OF WANDERING AWAITS US, SO LET'S GO!
NOW, THE HISTORIC POINTS OF INTEREST IN OUR FAIR TOWN ARE NOT LIMITED TO CHURCHES ALONE! NO SIREE, BOB!
WE'LL ALSO VISIT THE UNDERGROUND GRAPEFRUIT GROTTO, THE WESTSIDE SILENT DINNER THEATER, AND THE BIGGEST CAN-OPENER COLLECTION THIS SIDE OF THE MISSISSIPPI...

...NOT TO MENTION THE LOVELY GARDEN OF TALKING STATUES AT THE SPRINGFIELD FUNERAL HOME... OH, DEAR!
HEY!
DADDY! LOOK OUT!
JIMMINY CRICKET!
SCREEECH!
THUMP!
GOOD HEAVENS! WHAT HAVE I DONE?
IS IT LEVIATHAN CAST FROM THE SEA, DADDY?
GEE, I'M SORRY MISTER, I DIDN'T EVEN KNOW SHE WAS YOUR GAL...
DADDY, HE SMELLS LIKE THE OUTDOOR POTTY AT YOUTH CAMP!
NEVER MIND, TODD. UMPH! HE'S STILL ONE OF AHMPH! GOD'S CREATURES AND NEEDS OOPH! MEDICAL ATTENTION!
'SIDES, SHE TALKED TO ME FIRST...
NOW WHEN WE GET TO THE HOSPITAL, YOU BOYS LET ME DO ALL THE TALKING! I DON'T WANT ANYONE THINKING THAT THIS POOR MAN WAS IN ANY WAY RESPONSIBLE!
KWIK-E-M
HEY MATILDA! GIVE US A SMOOCH!
OH, MAMA! COULD MY TIMING GET ANY BETTER?

ALL RIGHT, NERD DUDE! PEEL OUT AND DRIVE FASTER THAN YOU'VE EVER DRIVEN BEFORE!
BOYS, AS LONG AS WE COOPERATE, EVERYTHING WILL BE OKILLY-DOKILLY!
OW!
BUT, DADDY, WE'RE SCARED!
BY THE RULES OF THE CONVENIENCE STORE CONVENTION, I PLACE YOU UNDER KWIK-E-MART ARREST! STOP THIS CAR AT ONCE!
KA-CLUMP!
YAAAAAH!
YOU ARE A BAD, BAD MAN, MR. GETAWAY DRIVER! YOU SHOULD KNOW THAT A HINDU MANAGER AND HIS MONEY ARE NOT SOON PARTED!
GETAWAY DRIVER?? NOW, THAT'S JUST CRAZY TALK!
KEEP THE PEDAL TO THE METAL, KEMOSABE, OR I'LL PUT SOME METAL IN YOUR NOODLE!
Springfield P.D.
Saturday 03/06
10:19 a.m.
WHOO-A! WHOO-A! WHOO-A!
LOOKS LIKE WE GOT US SOME JOY RIDERS HERE, LOU!
LET'S BRING EM DOWN A FEW NOTCHES.
YOU SAID IT, CHIEF!
WHOO-A! WHOO-A! WHOO-A!
BANG!
BANG!
PA-CHING!
PA-CHING!
DADDY, I THINK THE POLICE ARE SHOOTING AT US...
WHAT??! TH-THAT'S RI-DIDDILY-DICULOUS! H-HAVE THEY GONE INSANE?
LOOK OUT, LITTLE NERD DUDE!
BUMP!
...OOOOH!
BANG!
HEINOUS! I SHOT OUT THE TIRE OF MY OWN GETAWAY CAR!
HSSSSSSS!
Springfield P.D.
Saturday 03/06
10:20 a.m.
WHOO-A! WHOO-A! WHOO-A!
WE GOT 'EM NOW, LOU. THEY'VE LOST CONTROL OF THEIR VEHICLE! COME TA POPPA, YOU SCOFFLAWS!
YEAH, BUT CHIEF, IF YOU DON'T SLOW DOWN, WE MIGHT...

LORD, PROTECT US! WE'RE GOING TO...
CRASH!
THE FOLLOWING STORY YOU'VE JUST SEEN IS TRUE.
DUE TO ITS GRAPHIC NATURE, PARENTAL GUIDANCE IS SUGGESTED...WHICH IS SOMETHING WE PROBABLY SHOULD HAVE WARNED YOU ABOUT EARLIER...SORRY.
ANYWAY, HERE'S WHAT HAPPENED TO THE INDIVIDUALS INVOLVED...
SNAKE WAS LOCKED-DOWN IN A MAXIMUM SECURITY CELL AT THE SPRINGFIELD PRISON.
TWO HOURS LATER HE WAS SEEN BOARDING A FLIGHT TO MEXICO.
110968
APU RETRIEVED HIS STOLEN MONEY, WHICH AMOUNTED TO $25.17. WHILE THE KWIK-E-MART WAS LEFT UNATTENDED, A DISPLAY CASE FULL OF FROZEN YOGURT WAS STOLEN.
ROD FLANDERS HAD BRIDGEWORK AND A MINOR OPERATION TO REMOVE A CAMERA EYEPIECE FROM HIS EYE SOCKET.
FOR SIX MONTHS, TODD FLANDERS HAD TO BE DOWNGRADED FROM "BIG BOY" SHORTS TO PLASTIC PANTS AT BEDTIME.
CHIEF WIGGUM WAS FEATURED ON THE HIT FOX SPECIAL, "WHEN GOOD SNACKS GO BAD."
Springfield P.D. Saturday 03/06 10:45 a.m.
AND NED FLANDERS WON A LOCAL EMMY FOR HIS ENTERTAINING DOCUMENTARY-- BUT REFUSED THE AWARD, SAYING HE COULDN'T ACCEPT ANY GRAVEN IMAGES.
REPAIR ESTIMATE
END

SCRIPT JESSE LEON MCCANN · PENCILS PHIL ORTIZ · INKS TIM HARKINS · COLOR & LETTERS KAREN BATES · EDITOR BILL MORRISON

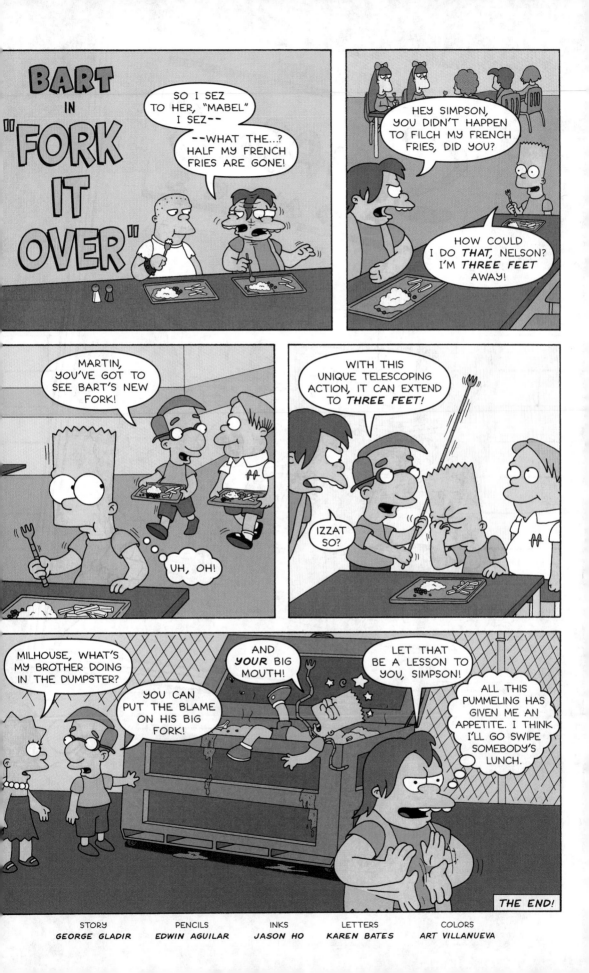

STORY
GEORGE GLADIR

PENCILS
EDWIN AGUILAR

INKS
JASON HO

LETTERS
KAREN BATES

COLORS
ART VILLANUEVA

FULL METAL JACKASS!
#54
US $2.50
CAN $3.50
SIMPSONS™
COMICS
...WHAT?
GROENING
Morrison
J.Ho

AAAAH!
CRASH!
SMASH!
TANKS for NOTHING
IAN BOOTHBY
SCRIPT
PHIL ORTIZ
PENCILS
TIM HARKINS
INKS
ART VILLANUEVA
COLORS
KAREN BATES
LETTERS
BILL MORRISON
EDITOR
MATT GROENING
PEACENIK

JUST A FRIENDLY REMINDER TO FILE YOUR TAXES ON TIME THIS YEAR!
WHA...AAH! MY HEART!
IRS
IRS
I'LL CALL AN AMBULANCE.
YOU'VE CHANGED, KYLE.
STEVE, YOU'RE AN IRS NINJA. THIS IS NOT PART OF OUR JOB.
LATER, AT SPRINGFIELD HOSPITAL...
SPRINGFIELD GENERAL HOSPITAL
THANKS FOR DOING MY BACK TAXES, LISA. CAN'T MAKE HEADS OR TAILS OF THOSE THINGS SINCE THEY BROUGHT IN THE NEW MATH.
IT'S MY PLEASURE. MY TEACHER MISS HOOVER GIVES ME EXTRA CREDIT FOR DOING HERS.
GRAMPA, DID YOU EVER RECEIVE YOUR VETERANS TAX BENEFIT?
NO.
WELL, YOU'RE OWED ABOUT FORTY YEARS WORTH, WHICH ACCORDING TO MY CALCULATIONS WOULD BE...
BEEP! BEEP! BEEP!
HOT DIGGETY!

LATER, AT A GOVERNMENT OFFICE...
WELL, MR. SIMPSON, IT'S A **RARE** CASE WHERE A GOVERNMENT AGENCY HAS MADE A **MISTAKE**.
SIR, WE BOMBED THE **WRONG** EMBASSY AGAIN.
I DON'T EVEN THINK THERE **IS** A **PRUSSIA** ANYMORE.
KELLY, IX-NAY IN FRONT OF THE IVILIAN-SAY!
NOW, MR. SIMPSON, YOU HAVE **TWO OPTIONS**. YOU COULD TAKE THIS **CHECK** FOR THE AMOUNT WE OWE YOU.
GIMME! GIMME! GIMME!
OR...
...WE COULD LET YOU TAKE THE ITEM OF YOUR **CHOICE** FROM OUR **WAREHOUSE!** ALL ITEMS THE GOVERNMENT NO LONGER HAS USE FOR.
NASA
SWEET MOTHER MCGILLICUTTY!
ROSWELL ALIENS
ROSWELL ALIENS
ROSWELL ALIENS
ROSWELL ALIENS
PRESIDENTIAL ROBOTS

TIME MACHINE PROTOTYPE DO NOT TOUCH!
ZZZZAP!
TRUST ME, YOU DON'T WANT TO TRY THIS MACHINE!
ZZZZAP!
COME ALONG SLAVE!
FWASH!
LET'S JUST FORGET WE SAW THAT, SHALL WE?
BETSY, IS THAT YOU?
YOU KNOW THIS TANK?
DROVE HER IN THE BIG WAR!
ARE YOU SURE?

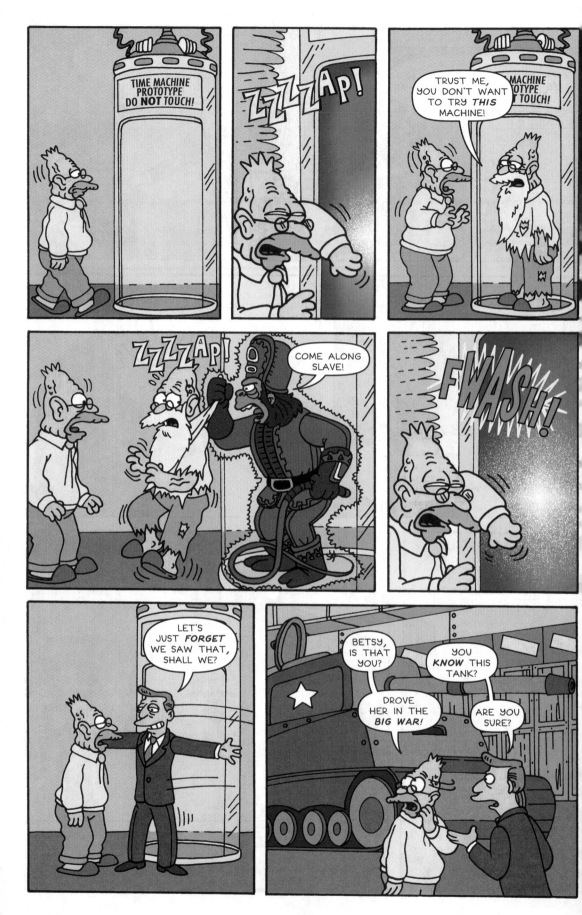

SEE THAT GOLF CLUB? THAT'S WHERE I RAN OVER BOB HOPE. YOUNGSTER WAS TOO SASSY FER MY LIKIN'!
SO, WILL YOU TAKE THE TANK AND FORGET THE DEBT?
MISTER, YOU GOT YOURSELF A DEAL!
THIS IS ARNIE PIE WITH THE MORNING TRAFFIC. ON I-15 THINGS ARE MOVING ALONG. I-16 LOOKS GOOD. BUT ON I-17 AVOID THE FLAMING WRECKAGE AND CRUSHED VEHICLES. OH, THE HUMANITY!
DRIVERS ARE ADVISED TO WATCH FOR THE SWERVING TANK WITH ITS RIGHT BLINKER ON, DRIVEN BY WHAT APPEARS TO BE GABBY HAYES!
OKAY, POPS, STEP OUT OF THE VEHICLE, AND LET'S SEE YOUR LICENSE!

WELL, YOUR DRIVER'S LICENSE EXPIRED A LONG TIME AGO, BUT YOUR TANK DRIVING LEARNER'S PERMIT IS STILL VALID.
LOOK, I'LL LET YOU OFF WITH A WARNING. BUT CAN YOU DO ME A FAVOR?
SOON, AT CITY HALL...
THOOM!!
CUTBACK ON THE POLICE SLUSH FUND, WILL YA, QUIMBY?
WIGGUM! I'LL HAVE YOUR BADGE FOR THIS!
JOE QUIMBY
YEAH, WELL I'LL HAVE TO FIND IT FIRST!
LATER...
IT'S NOT FAIR! HOW COME GRAMPA GETS A TANK, AND I CAN'T EVEN GET ACCESS TO NERVE GAS?
NOW, BART. I DON'T LIKE THE GENEVA CONVENTION ANY MORE THAN YOU DO.

I CAN'T BELIEVE YOU'D EVEN ALLOW SUCH A WEAPON OF DEATH AND DESTRUCTION TO SIT IN OUR **DRIVEWAY**!
HEY, IF IT WEREN'T FOR TANKS LIKE THAT ONE DEFENDING THIS COUNTRY, YOU'D BE SPEAKING **AUSTRALIAN**!
LISA'S RIGHT, DAD. I CAN'T STAND BY AND WATCH YOU CRUSH THE TOWN IN YOUR TANK.
WILL YOU DRIVE IT WITH ME?
YOU **GOT** IT!
DAD!
LISA, I SAID I WOULDN'T **STAND** BY. IN THE TANK, I'LL BE **SITTING**.
MY LEARNER'S PERMIT SAYS I NEED A **RESPONSIBLE ADULT** IN THE TANK WITH ME.
WELL, THAT'S **ME** ALL RIGHT!
GRRR! LOUSY NONFROST-FREE FRIDGE. OPEN UP AND GIVE ME MY ICE CREAM!
A LITTLE **HAMMERING** WILL GET RID OF THAT ICE!
AS SOON AS THE FREON GAS CLEARS, I'LL GET MY HAT, AND WE'LL **HIT THE TOWN**!

SOON...
DRINK Duff BEER
EIGHT BALL IN THE CORNER POCKET!
KRUSTYBURGER
MENU
YOU FORGOT THE FRIES LAST TIME!
THEY'RE IN THERE *THIS* TIME, SIR. I *PROMISE!*
WHOA, DUDE! SUDDENLY MY MASCULINITY FEELS *SO* THREATENED.
CRACKLES

THE NEXT MORNING...
THAT WAS FUN, SON. NOW, IF YOU COULD JUST PARK BETSY AROUND BACK.
CAN'T, DAD! I'M *LATE* FOR WORK. GOTTA TAKE THE TANK! BARELY ENOUGH TIME TO CHANGE MY CLOTHES.
SPRINGFIELD RETIREMENT CASTLE
WHAT'S THAT YOU'RE WEARING ANYWAY?
A *TANK TOP*. WHEN ELSE AM I GONNA HAVE AN EXCUSE TO WEAR ONE? GOTTA GO!
SOON...
SPRINGFIELD NUCLEAR POWER PLANT
EMPLOYEE PARKING ONLY

SMITHERS, IS THAT A V-67 ***SHERWOOD TANK***?
I'LL HAVE TO DOUBLE CHECK MY TIME LIFE BOOKS, SIR, BUT I'D SAY "YES."

AH, THAT TAKES ME BACK.

MEANWHILE, IN THE NEXT TOWN OVER...
SHELBYVILLE NUCLEAR POWER PLANT
EMPLOYEE PARKING ONLY

FREDERICKS, LOOK AT THE SATELLITE SPY-CAM FEED FROM THE SPRINGFIELD PLANT'S PARKING LOT. IS THAT A V-67 SHERWOOD TANK?
I BELIEVE IT IS, MR. AMADOPOLIS.
SO THAT TWO-FACED JANUS, MONTY BURNS, HAS BROKEN THE ARMS TREATY.
SPRINGF
UCLEAR POW
YOU SEE, SMITHERS, I WASN'T ALWAYS THE MIDDLE-AGED MAN YOU SEE BEFORE YOU.
I USED TO BE THE LEADER OF A SPRINGFIELD GANG. I KNOW IT MUST BE HARD IMAGINING ME CLAD HEAD TO TOE IN LEATHER.
I SAY, AMADOPOLIS, YOUR TOWN, SHELBYVILLE, HAS A WEAK POLITICAL SYSTEM AND INEPT SANITATION MANAGEMENT.
YES, WELL SPRINGFIELD HAS A MEDIOCRE POST-SECONDARY EDUCATION FACILITY AND POOR TAX INCENTIVES FOR THE UPPER MIDDLE CLASS.

THAT'S IT! I CHALLENGE YOU TO BATTLE!
I DIDN'T THINK YOU HAD THE OLIVES!
LET'S GET READY TO RUUUUUUUUUUUMBLE!
OF COURSE, BEING MILLIONAIRES, WE HIRED OTHERS TO DO THE ACTUAL FIGHTING. MOSTLY ARMIES NOT BUSY WITH WARS OF THEIR OWN.
DIE, BELGIUM!
EAT HOT WAFFLES, CANADA!

"WE GOT OLDER, ARMIES GOT MORE PRICEY, AND THE SLAUGHTER OF INNOCENTS LOST ITS APPEAL. WE SIGNED A TREATY AND WENT OUR SEPARATE WAYS."
SPAIN
WALES
ITALY
INDIA
MEXICO
UNITED STATES OF AMERICA
SUDAN
TREATY
WELL, THAT'S ENOUGH REMINISCING. START MY CAR WILL YOU, SMITHERS?
SMITHERS?
MMMM... HEAD TO TOE IN LEATHER.
THAT AFTERNOON...
HEY, HOMER! WE MADE A HANG GLIDER OUT OF PILLOW-CASES AND POPSICLE STICKS. WATCH ME TEST IT OUT!
HMMMM. I DON'T KNOW, BOY. BETTER LET MILHOUSE TRY IT FIRST!

HEY, MARGE! WHAT'S FOR DINNER? ⁝SNIFF⁝ ⁝SNIFF⁝ SMELLS LIKE...
AAAAH!
ME!
WHAT ARE YOU DOING HERE? IT'S NOT THE THIRD SUNDAY OF THE MONTH.
I AIN'T HERE FOR DINNER. I WANT MY TANK!
OH, NOW IT'S YOUR TANK, IS IT?
IT'S ALWAYS BEEN MY TANK!
THAT'S NOT HOW I REMEMBER IT.
YOU KNOW, FOR YOU, SENILITY WILL BE LIKE SLIPPING INTO A WARM, FAMILIAR BATH.
IT'S SELMA ON THE PHONE. SHE SAYS TO TURN TO CHANNEL FIVE! NOW!
THERE'S EARTH-SHAKING NEWS!
DID THEY RENEW "HARSH REALM"?
NO, WE'RE AT WAR WITH SHELBYVILLE!

WAR! HUH! GOOD GOD, Y'ALL! WHAT IS IT GOOD FOR?
WE ASKED MAYOR QUIMBY.
KENT
I, ER...AH, HAVE BEEN INFORMED THAT AS OF NOON TODAY, SHELBYVILLE, UNDER THE ADVICE OF ARISTOTLE AMADOPOLIS, HAS **DECLARED WAR** ON SPRINGFIELD.
THERE IS **NO REASON** TO **PANIC,** AND I'LL BE BACK FROM MY **VACATION** TO...AH... UM...WHEREVER...AS SOON AS POSSIBLE.
BLAME FOR THIS IS BEING PLACED IN THE WRINKLED LAP OF MONTGOMERY BURNS, WHO APPARENTLY **BROKE** THE **"NO WEAPONS ARRANGEMENT"** OF THE **"TWO RICH PUNKS TREATY"**.
POINTING THE FINGER
KENT
"SHELBYVILLE HAS RESPONDED BY **STOCKPILING** GROUND, AIR, AND NUCLEAR WEAPONS."
SHELBYVILLE NUCLEAR POWER PLANT
IF IT'S A FIGHT MONTGOMERY BURNS WANTS, WE SHALL SOON SEE WHO IS ZEUS AND WHO IS MERELY ODIN!
I DIDN'T GO LOOKING FOR A FIGHT, BUT IF MY FRIEND **IS** SPOILING FOR A SCUFFLE, I'M JUST THE JAKE TO GIVE IT TO HIM. WE WILL NOT STOP UNTIL THE STREETS RUN **RED WITH BLOOD!**
OR IF BLOOD IS UNAVAILABLE, THEN SWEAT, TEARS, OR A **GENERIC BLOOD SUBSTITUTE**.

CAN THEY DO THAT? CAN TWO BUSINESSMEN DECLARE WAR AND DRAG THEIR TOWNS WITH THEM?
DING DONG!
LOUSY CAPITALISM!
HEY, IF YOU DON'T LIKE IT, MOVE TO RUSSIA!
GASP!
HELLO, STRANGER. I'VE COME TO INFORM YOU THAT A NUCLEAR MISSILE HAS BEEN MOUNTED ON YOUR FRONT LAWN, AND YOU'RE NOW A VIABLE MILITARY TARGET. THANKS FOR DOING YOUR PART FOR THE WAR EFFORT!
OH, WELL, AT LEAST FLANDERS WILL BE IMPRESSED.
D'OH!
DON'T WORRY, MOM. EVERYONE KNOWS YOU CAN'T WIN A NUCLEAR WAR. NO ONE WILL DARE FIRE THE FIRST SHOT.

SOON...
GRONK!
SKREE!
BOOM!
BART, PUT THAT DOWN AND HELP ME THINK OF A WAY TO STOP THIS MADNESS!
GAME GUY
BOOM!
SKREE!
I DUNNO, LIS. STOPPING CARNAGE AND DESTRUCTION KINDA GOES AGAINST THE GRAIN FOR ME.

SHELBYVILLE CITIZEN, ARISTOTLE AMADOPOLIS, DECLARED TODAY THAT UNLESS SPRINGFIELD **DISMANTLES** ITS ARSENAL BY **MIDNIGHT TONIGHT**, THEY WILL PLUNGE US INTO **FULL GLOBAL THERMONUCLEAR WAR**.
AS SEEN IN THAT REALLY COOL MATTHEW BRODERICK FILM.
MISSILE CRISIS
KENT
I'M SORRY IT HAD TO COME TO THIS, KENT, BUT WE'VE ALL LED LONG HAPPY LIVES, AND **I WILL NOT BACK DOWN!** DO YOUR WORST, ARI!
WE HERE AT CHANNEL 6 ADVISE YOU TO USE YOUR **REMAINING TIME** TO **MAKE PEACE** WITH YOUR **LOVED ONES**.
MISSIL
SHA-BOOM KA-BOOM cafe

SLEEP-EAZY MOTEL
HOURLY RATES ADULT MOVIES
CONFOUND IT, SMITHERS. IT'S TEN MINUTES TO MIDNIGHT. WE'RE AT WAR. WHAT ARE WE DOING AT A ONE STAR MOTEL?
THEY GAVE THE BEST ROOM RATES FOR...
...AN INTERVENTION!
¡GASP!¡ YOU!
¡GASP!¡ YOU!
SMITHERS, HOW COULD YOU?
WELL, IT WAS THE LITTLE GIRL'S IDEA.
BUT I'M SORRY, SIR, I DRAW THE LINE AT CAUSING ARMAGEDDON.
THIS WILL NOT LOOK GOOD ON YOUR PERMANENT RECORD.
DON'T YOU SEE? YOU CAN'T DESTROY TWO CITIES BECAUSE OF YOUR HATRED FOR ONE ANOTHER.
HOW COULD I HATE GOOD OLD MONTY?
HATRED? I DON'T HATE ARI!
THEN WHAT STARTED ALL THIS?
HE INSULTED SHELBYVILLE!
HE INSULTED SPRINGFIELD!
YOU TWO TURN MY STOMACH. IN MY DAY, WHICH WAS ALSO YOUR DAY, WE DIDN'T NEED SISSY WEAPONS TO SETTLE AN ARGUMENT. WE'D FIGHT IT OUT ONE ON ONE, MAN TO MAN!
THE SMELLY OLD FELLOW IS RIGHT.
LET'S SETTLE THIS ONCE AND FOR ALL, HONORABLY, MAN TO MAN!
SMITHERS!
FREDERICKS!
GO FIGHT!

LATER...
Millionaire's Club
NO GAME SHOW WINNERS ALLOWED
SIR! THE FIGHT IS OVER!
THE WINNER IS...
COAT CHECK
NOT NOW, SMITHERS! IS THAT THE FINAL BID FOR THE WEAPONS STOCKPILE? GOING, GOING...
...SOLD TO HANK SCORPIO!
WELL, THAT'S JUST FANTASTIC. YOU'VE MADE MY DAY! NO HARD FEELINGS, DR. COLOSSUS?
KILL SUPE
AAGH! WHAT A WEEK I'M HAVING!
DON'T YOU CARE WHO WON, SIR?
AH, SMITHERS, IN WAR THERE ARE NO WINNERS. THE ONLY VICTORS ARE THE PEACE-MAKERS AND THE WAR PROFITEERS.
WE WON, SIR.
EXCELLENT!

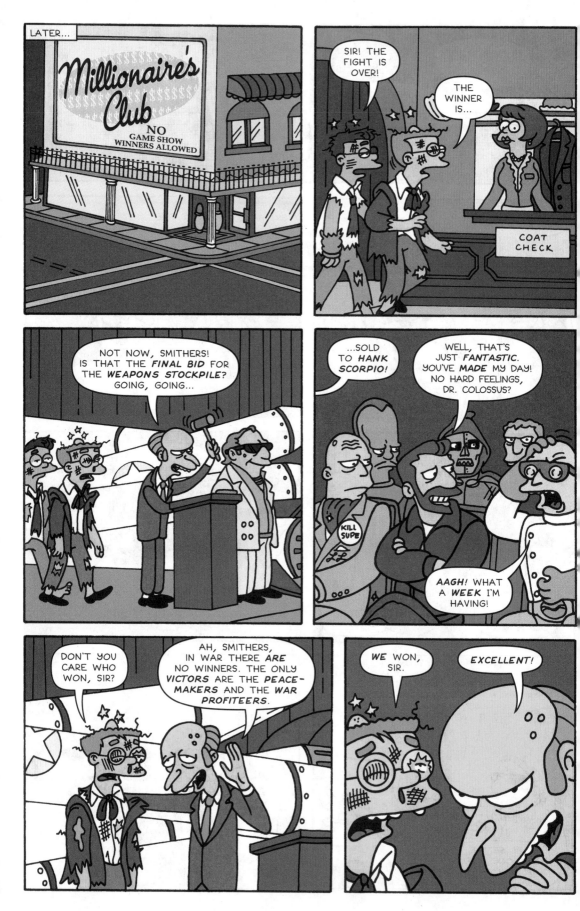

LATER...
WELL, I'M GLAD THAT'S OVER.
MOSTLY OVER. THE GOVERNMENT WAS SO UPSET AT AN ATOMIC CIVIL WAR BREAKING OUT BETWEEN NEIGHBORING TOWNS THAT THEY'VE BANNED THE CITY'S USE OF NUCLEAR MATERIALS FOR SIX MONTHS.
BUT WHERE WILL OUR POWER COME FROM?
REMEMBER ⁝GASP⁝ IF I HAVE ANOTHER HEART ATTACK ⁝WHEEZE⁝, WAKE ME FOR LUNCH!
WE REALLY NEED A BETTER UNION.
YOU NEVER FAIL TO AMAZE ME, SIR.
THANK YOU, SMITHERS. NOW WASH YOUR HANDS AND GET BACK IN YOUR WHEEL. YOUR WOODCHIP BREAK IS OVER!
THE END

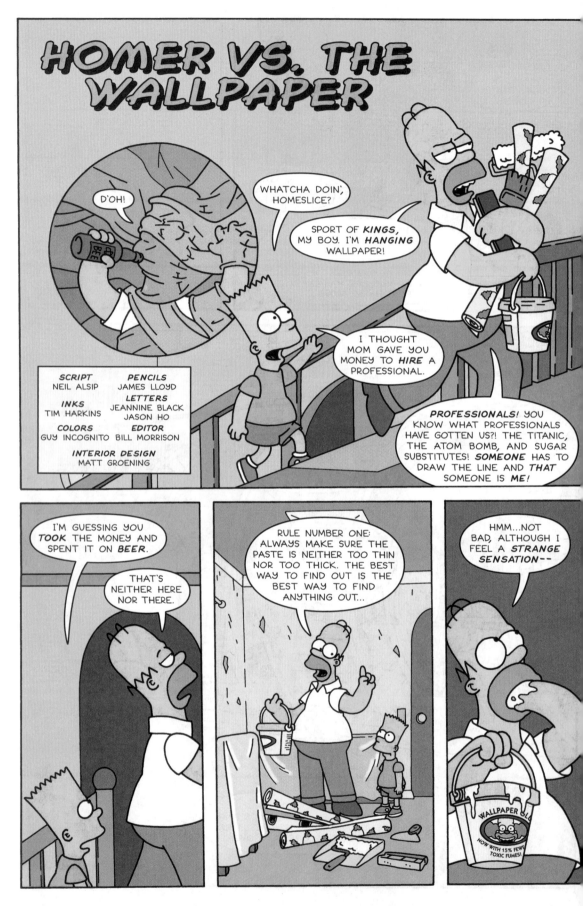

HOMER VS. THE WALLPAPER

D'OH!

WHATCHA DOIN', HOMESLICE?

SPORT OF *KINGS*, MY BOY. I'M *HANGING* WALLPAPER!

I THOUGHT MOM GAVE YOU MONEY TO *HIRE* A PROFESSIONAL.

SCRIPT
NEIL ALSIP

PENCILS
JAMES LLOYD

INKS
TIM HARKINS

LETTERS
JEANNINE BLACK
JASON HO

COLORS
GUY INCOGNITO

EDITOR
BILL MORRISON

INTERIOR DESIGN
MATT GROENING

PROFESSIONALS! YOU KNOW WHAT PROFESSIONALS HAVE GOTTEN US?! THE TITANIC, THE ATOM BOMB, AND SUGAR SUBSTITUTES! *SOMEONE* HAS TO DRAW THE LINE AND *THAT* SOMEONE IS *ME!*

I'M GUESSING YOU *TOOK* THE MONEY AND SPENT IT ON *BEER*.

THAT'S NEITHER HERE NOR THERE.

RULE NUMBER ONE: ALWAYS MAKE SURE THE PASTE IS NEITHER TOO THIN NOR TOO THICK. THE BEST WAY TO FIND OUT IS THE BEST WAY TO FIND ANYTHING OUT...

HMM...NOT BAD, ALTHOUGH I FEEL A *STRANGE* SENSATION--

WALLPAPER GL[...]
NOW WITH 15% FEWE[R]
TOXIC FUMES!

BEE BOO BEE BOO BEE BOO BEE BOO BEE BOO
AN HOUR AFTER THE BOWEL DE-GLUING...
NOW THAT WE HAVE THAT LITTLE UNPLEASANTNESS OUT OF THE WAY, IT'S TIME TO CUT THE WALL-PAPER TO SIZE.
JUST EVEN IT UP A LITTLE...TAKE A TEENSY BIT OFF HERE...HMM... NOT QUITE EVEN. MAYBE A PEENSY BIT OFF THERE...
OKAY, THEN A TEENSY MORE HERE, PEENSY MORE THERE...STILL NOT RIGHT. TEENSY MORE...PEENSY MORE...TEENSY!... PEENSY!
YAAAARGH!!
NOW WE'LL SEE WHO'S BOSS!

BEE BOO BEE BOO BEE BOO BEE BOO BEE BOO
NOW THEN, --SHUT UP, BOY-- IT'S TIME TO PUT THE ***STUPID*** WALLPAPER ON THE ***STUPID*** WALL. SO LET'S ALL JUST REMAIN ***CALM,*** NOTHING TO SEE HERE PEOPLE...
JUST SMOOSH IT OVER AND...
ARRGGHH!
SON OF A ✩#@!!
SWEET CHILD OF @✩$!!
I'M GONNA @#$% YOU STUPID $%#$#✩!!!
✩%$# SWEET GALLOPING HONEYBAKED $%✩#@%$# @%✩@#$@%#%@$% $@%#$@%%!!!!

YOU'RE RUNNING OUT OF CURSES! SWITCH TO CHINESE!
去你
GREAT BIG BOOK OF CHINESE SWEARING
該死
DIE! DIE! DIE! DIE!
SOON...
HOLY 狗屎
LATER...
HEY, HOMEFRIES. EITHER YOU'VE FINALLY SNAPPED, OR YOU BROKE DOWN AND HIRED A PRO.
NO, SON, AS I LAY THERE COVERED IN WALLPAPER AND SHAME, I THOUGHT BACK TO OUR FOREFATHERS, THE PIONEERS THAT TOILED AND SLAVED TO MAKE THIS GREAT COUNTRY WHAT IT IS TODAY, AND I ASKED, WHAT WOULD THEY HAVE DONE?
SO?
I HIRED A DRIFTER.
OKAY, NOW ALL I NEED IS A SPONGE, SOME WET RAGS...OH, AND YOUR ATM NUMBER.
3144, MY MAN, 3144.
THE END

Picture Perfect

KWIK-E-MART
KWIK-E-MART PARKING ONLY
Duff BEER 12.95
KWIK-E-MART PARKING ONLY
WHAT'S GOING ON?
IT WOULD APPEAR AS THOUGH SOMEONE HAS RESPECTED MY FRONT WINDOW NOT AT ALL. THIS WOULD NOT BE THE FIRST TIME THAT MY BELOVED KWIK-E-MART HAS HAD THIS DISRESPECT TAGGED UPON ITS PERSON.
WE'VE HAD IT AT THE POWER PLANT AS WELL.
AND I'VE SEEN IT AT MY HOME!
SPRINGFIELD ELEMENTARY SCHOOL
WE'VE HAD IT AT THE SCHOOL TOO!

MEANWHILE...
OK, BART, YOU DO YOUR LITTLE WHEELIES. BUT ALL THE ATTENTION IS GOING TO BE ON ME, WHEN I WIN THE BIG ART CONTEST.
SPRING
WHATCHA PAINTING? THE ALONE-A-LISA?
HEY! BART! GIVE THAT BACK!
HEY, LOOK AT ME! I'M A BIG ART GEEK!
@#%*!!
JUST YOU WAIT, BART. JUST YOU WAIT.
THE NEXT DAY...
WHAT AN INTERESTING COMMENTARY ON HOW A LARCENOUS SOCIETY IS STEALING OUR COLLECTIVE SOUL.
HA, HA! ER...I MEAN... THANKS.
REVOFLOV
WELCOME
THE SKINNER FAMILY
Our Lovely School
DANGER!
WHY ISN'T ANYONE LOOKING AT MY PAINTING?
OH, WELL. MIGHT AS WELL GO AND SEE WHAT THE OTHER KIDS HAVE DONE.

HMMM. THE LINES ARE FRAUDULENT. THE COLORS ARE ODALISQUE. THERE'S A BODACIOUS USE OF NEGATIVE SPACE. BUT IT SEEMS TO BE MISSING SOMETHING. I WONDER WHAT THAT COULD BE? HEH, HEH.
SOON...
I WONDER WHAT THE FUSS IS? WAIT, THAT'S MY PAINTING!
WELL, THIS IS GENIUS! THE COMMENTARY OF HOW INNOCENCE CAN BE SO EASILY CORRUPTED, INFLUENCED AND INFRINGED UPON BY THE DECAY OF MODERN DAY SOCIETY IS FABULOUS.
HI. THIS IS MINE. I DID IT. I'M THE ARTIST.
WELL, UM, THANK YOU. I MEAN, IT'S A PAINTING OF THE SCHOOL...
I'M AWARDING IT FIRST PRIZE!
WHAT?!
AND HERE'S THE FIRST PRIZE CHECK!
WHAT THE...??!!
WHAT? YOU'RE THE ONE WHO'S BEEN DOING THIS?
SO THAT'S **YOUR** MARK?
LISA?
NO! WAIT! THERE'S BEEN A MISUNDERSTANDING!

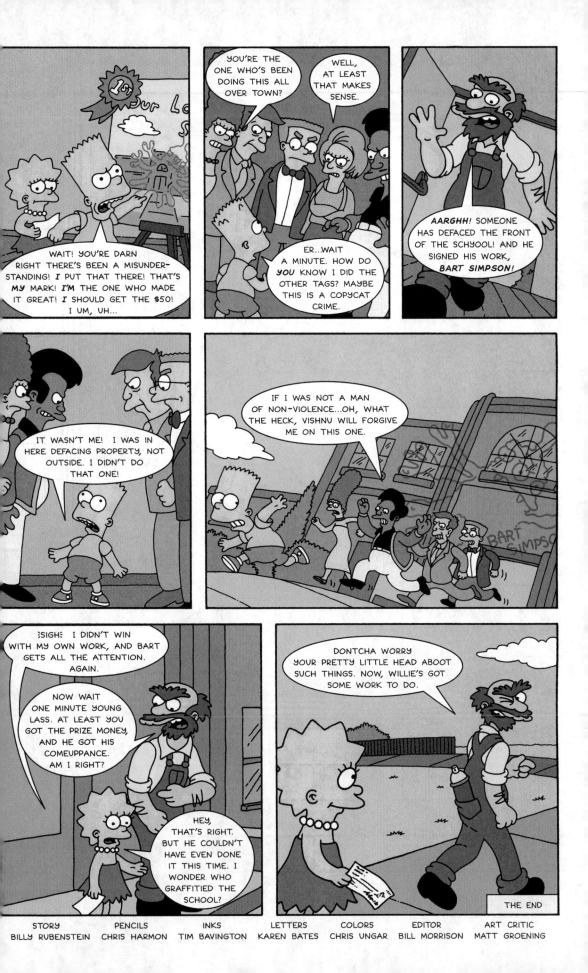

STORY
BILLY RUBENSTEIN

PENCILS
CHRIS HARMON

INKS
TIM BAVINGTON

LETTERS
KAREN BATES

COLORS
CHRIS UNGAR

EDITOR
BILL MORRISON

ART CRITIC
MATT GROENING

SIEGE THE DAY!
SIMPSONS COMICS
#55
US $2.50
CAN $3.50
©2001 BONGO ENTERTAINMENT, INC. THE SIMPSONS ©&TM TWENTIETH CENTURY FOX FILM CORPORATION. ALL RIGHTS RESERVED.
THE TEN COMMANDMENTS

SIEGE on
EVERGREEN TERRACE
YOU SCAMPERING PUP! I WAS ON THE SHORES OF NORMANDY, THE HILLS OF IWO JIMA, AND THE FRONT LINES OF WATERLOO!
I DON'T CARE WHERE YOU WENT ON YOUR LAST VACATION, AMERICAN SWINE! YOU DON'T FRIGHTEN ME! MAKE YOUR MOVE!
KLIK!
JESSE LEON MCANN SCRIPT
PHIL ORTIZ PENCILS
TIM BAVINGTON INKS
ART VILLANUEVA COLORS
KAREN BATES LETTERS
BILL MORRISON EDITOR
MATT GROENING TOWEL BOY

"F-6"
"YOU SUNK MY BATTLESHIP!"
BAA-BOOOOOM!!
"EXCELLENT"
GOOD THING WE HAVE A BEACH IN THIS STATE, IF WE'RE GONNA HAVE HEAT-WAVES LIKE THIS!
SINCE IT'S BEEN SO HOT, I'M HAPPY HAVING A STATE BEACH!
WHY IS EVERY-ONE TALKING? YOU CAN'T HEAR EACH OTHER WITH HEAD-PHONES ON!
Blue Seagull Reserve
PLEASE WATCH OUT FOR OUR ENDANGERED FRIENDS
STOP FEEDING THEM POP-ROCKS!
IT SURE IS NICE LIVING IN A STATE WITH A BEACH DURING THIS HOT WEATHER!
I'VE GOT AN IDEA! LET'S GO SWIM-MING! I MEAN, WHAT ARE STATE BEACHES FOR, ANYWAY?
HOMEY, THAT'S A WONDERFUL IDEA--IT BEING SO HOT AND ALL.
WOW! THE BEACH IS EMPTY! WHERE DID EVERY-BODY GO?
WHO CARES? I CAN'T WAIT TO DIP MY TOOTSIES IN THAT COOL, REFRESHING WATER!
WHOO! WHOO! WHOO! WHOO!
YOU THERE! THIS IS AN EMERGENCY SITUATION! STEP AWAY FROM THE SURF!
AHHH! HELP! I'VE GONE BLIND AND COMATOSE ...AGAIN!

SOON...
MY CORNS ARE BLISTERING, AND THERE'S SAND BETWEEN THE OLD BUM-CHEEKS!
I'M SO MAD WE GOT KICKED OFF THE BEACH, I'M BURNING UP! IN A HEAT WAVE, NO LESS!
STATE BEACH 1 MILE
I JUST WISH I KNEW WHO WAS BEHIND THIS!!
EWWW!
WELL, THAT WAS A JOLLY DIVERSION! WHAT GAME SHALL WE PLAY NEXT TO OCCUPY US ON A LAZY SATURDAY AFTERNOON?
SOUTH-EAST ASIA ROOM.
HOW ABOUT "CHARLIE AND THE YANK", SIR?
UNDER THE GENEVA CONVENTION, I RESPECTFULLY REQUEST MORE COCKROACHES WITH MY SPOILED RICE, MR. VC DEVIL, SIR!
GUM SOO MAO! MAO!
MEANWHILE...
I'M STILL SO ANGRY, I COULD KILL ABOUT A THOUSAND BLUE-HAIRED SEAGULLS!
OH, GET OVER IT, HOMER! YOU'VE GOT THE WHOLE FAMILY KEEPING YOU COOL.
DAD, THERE'S NOTHING YOU CAN DO ABOUT THE WEATHER.
LOUSY SUN...
DING DONG!
I'LL GET IT!
SCHRLICK!

WHAT DO YOU WANT?
HI, BUDDY. I'M CHUCK BLY, THE POOL GUY!
I'VE COME TO...DO YOU ALWAYS ANSWER THE DOOR WITH YOUR UNDERWEAR STUCK TO A BLOCK OF ICE?
I MIGHT.
ANYWAY, I'M HERE TO INSTALL THE POOL YOU ORDERED.
I ORDERED NO POOL, SIR. AWAY WITH YOU!
INVOICE
UH, ACCORDING TO THIS INVOICE, YOU DID. "ONE KING-SIZE, DELUXE OLYMPIC SWIMMING POOL," PAID FOR IN CASH.
IF I'D ORDERED A POOL, I'D CERTAINLY REMEMBER IT! I'M NOT AN IDIOT, YOU KNOW!
CLUNK!
ALL RIGHT. I GUESS SOMEBODY AT THE OFFICE MADE A MISTAKE.
I'LL JUST TAKE MY RIG AND GO HOME. TAKE IT EASY, MR. FLANDERS!
INDEED. GOOD DAY TO YOU.

FLANDERS?!!
OH, THAT SWIMMING POOL!
LOOK, FAMILY! THESE NICE MEN HAVE COME TO PUT AN OLYMPIC SWIMMING POOL IN OUR BACK YARD!
YAY!
POOL GUY
POOL GUY
OH, HOMIE, IT'S WONDERFUL! BUT HOW CAN WE AFFORD IT?
DON'T WORRY ABOUT A THING, MARGE...I MEAN, MRS. FLANDERS, IT'S ALL PAID FOR. SOON WE'LL BE FLOATING IN LIQUID LUXURY!
DID YOU JUST CALL ME MRS. FLANDERS?
MAAAARGE, QUIET! DON'T EMBARRASS ME IN FRONT OF THE POOL GUY!
THAT'S OKAY, I WASN'T LISTENING. I'VE ALREADY FIGURED IT'S BEST TO IGNORE YOU. SIGN HERE.
WOO-HOO! I LIKE THE WAY YOU THINK, POOL GUY!
YO.
INVOICE
LET ME INTRODUCE MY NEPHEW, BUCK BLY, ASSISTANT-TO-THE-POOL GUY. HE'LL BE YOUR LIAISON WITH US 'CAUSE, FRANKLY, I'M ALREADY SICK OF YOU.
ONE WEEK LATER...
GASP!
FHHHSSSSSS!
GASP!
FHHHSSSSSS!
GASP!
FHHHSSSSSS!
THIS IS KNUS NEWS. AND NOW THE WEATHER. HOPE YOU'RE READY FOR ANOTHER SCORCHER TODAY...
ARE WE EVER! RIGHT, BALDY? HEE HEE HEE!

GOGGLES? CHECK! NOSE PROTECTION? CHECK! LEMONADE? CHECK!
EVERYTHING I NEED FOR A PERFECT DAY BY THE POOL!
D'OH! AREN'T YOU DONE YET??
WE JUST TOLD YOU FIVE MINUTES AGO, NO! WE'RE WAITIN' FOR THE BUILDING INSPECTOR. EVERYTHING HAS TO BE IN ACCORDANCE WITH THE RULES OF THE SPRINGFIELD POOL BUILDERS AND FAST-FOOD FRY-COOKS UNION.
A FEW DAYS LATER...
NOPE, NOT YET.
D'OH!
ANOTHER COUPLE OF DAYS...
NO, SORRY.
D'OH!
FINALLY...
CONGRATULATIONS, BUDDY. YOUR POOL IS FINALLY DONE!
WOO-HOO!
DON'T FORGET TO FILL IT UP WITH WATER!
D'OH!!!

LATER...
NUTS! IT'S TOO CROWDED. SOMEBODY'S GONNA HAVE TO GET OUT!
SHUT UP, CHUNKY! YOU'RE NO CALLISTA SHOPCART YOURSELF!
JUDGING BY YOUR TOTAL MASS VERSUS WATER BUOYANCY AND VOLUME, I'D SAY **SEVERAL DOZEN** BODIES WILL HAVE TO GET OUT.
DOGGONE IT! I LOST MY CHOMPERS AGAIN!
SNAP!
RALPH HAS HIS NOSE STUCK IN THE FILTER AGAIN, MRS. SIMPSON!
EEEEEEEK!
HRRRRRMMMMM!

C'MON, POINDEXTER! IT'S TIME TO GO BUNGEE SWIMMING!
O-OKAY.
SPLOOSH!
HAW! HAW!
GLUB! MY TRUNKS! GLUB!
MAN, I'VE BEEN DYIN' TO SOAK THESE TIRED DOGS!
KER-SPLAASH!
OUT OF THE WAY, KIDS! MATURE ADULTS COMING THROUGH!
OH, I'VE SEEN ONE OF THESE BEFORE! HERE, LET ME ATTACH IT TO YOUR SUIT, BUDDY.
OKAY!
HI-DILLY-HO, HOMER! I-I JUST GOT BACK FROM A SUMMER RETREAT WITH THE BOYS AND I COULDN'T HELP BUT NOTICE THAT YOU'VE HAD A POOL BUILT IN YOUR BACKYARD.
THAT'S RIGHT, FLANDERS. WHAT ABOUT IT?

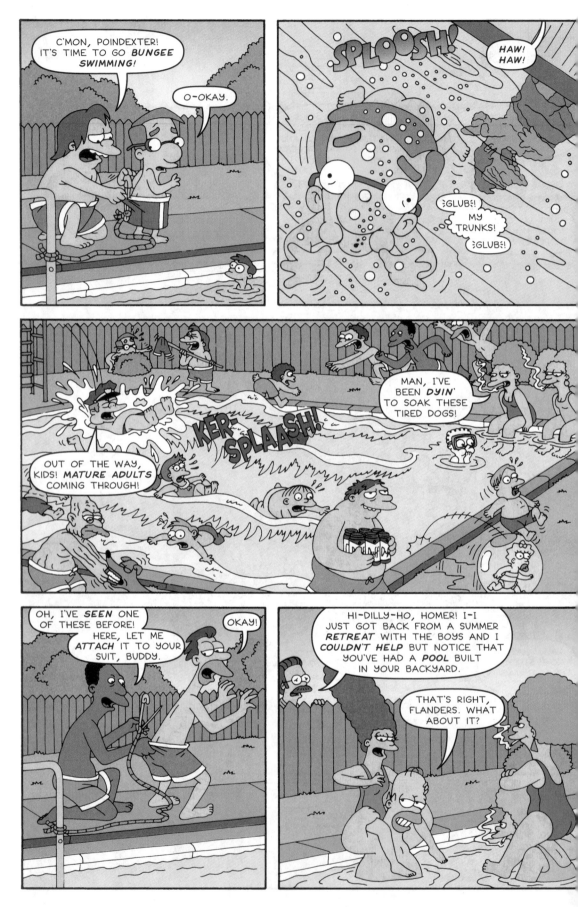

W-WELL, SIR, THE THING IS, I WAS SUPPOSED TO HAVE A POOL BUILT IN MY YARD WHILE I WAS GONE, AND THERE DOESN'T SEEM TO BE ONE THERE!
LISTEN FLANDERS, I CAN'T WORRY ABOUT THINGS THAT GO MISSING FROM YOUR YARD! YOU SHOULD CHAIN THINGS DOWN, LIKE I DO WITH MY LAWN GNOMES.
IT'S NOT THAT...
ARE YOU INFERRING THAT THIS IS YOUR POOL? WELL, IF THIS WAS YOUR POOL, WHAT WOULD IT BE DOING IN MY BACKYARD??
THAT'S WHAT I'D LIKE TO KNOW!
GASP! IT'S CHUCK BLY...
...POOL GUY. YEAH, YEAH.
LISTEN BUDDY, YOU'VE STOLEN MR. FLANDERS POOL AND WE'RE TAKING IT BACK!
THAT IS, UNLESS YOU WANT TO BUY IT LEGALLY.
WHAT? HOW DARE YOU EMBARRASS ME IN FRONT OF MY DISTINGUISHED GUESTS?!
BESIDES, YOU CAN'T REPOSSESS A POOL.
NO, BUT WE CAN FILL IT IN! I'LL BE BACK WITH THE DIRT TRUCKS!
JUST WANTED TO CLEAR THAT UP! TOODLE-DOO!
I'D LIKE TO SEE YOU TRY! YOU'LL HAVE TO BURY ME FIRST!
OH, NO! WHAT AM I GOING TO DO?? I'VE GOT TO THINK QUICK!

LISTEN CAREFULLY! I WANT TO PLACE **A VERY IMPORTANT** ORDER.
TWO EXTRA-LARGE HAM AND BACON PIZZAS WITH EXTRA CHEESE, AND I WANT THE CHEESE SPREAD **ALL THE WAY** TO THE EDGES OF THE CRUST. YOU GOT THAT?
YES, SIR!
NOW, A QUICK CALL TO **HERMAN** SHOULD TAKE CARE OF THE REST.
EVENTUALLY...
WHAT DO YOU MEAN WE **CAN'T LEAVE?** I GOT A QUICHE IN THE OVEN!
PEOPLE! THIS IS FOR YOUR **OWN PROTECTION!** SOME **VERY BAD MEN** ARE COMING AND I NEED HUMAN SHIELDS ...ER, **WITNESSES!**
JUST GO **BACK** INTO THE POOL.
HERMAN'S MILITARY ANTIQUES AND STAND-OFF RENTALS
V-DAY
B-BUT MR. SIMPSON, I THINK I'VE SPENT **TOO MUCH** TIME IN THE POOL TODAY ALREADY.
DON'T ARGUE WITH ME, MR. MOLEMAN!
MR. MOLEMAN? I'M **MILHOUSE!**

HOMER! THE GUESTS SAY YOU'RE HAVING ANOTHER ONE OF YOUR PATENTED "JERK" EPISODES.
DID YOU REFUSE TO LET THEM LEAVE??
CAN'T TALK NOW, MARGE! WE'RE ABOUT TO MEET THE ENEMY, AND THE ENEMY IS...
...THUS! ER, THEM!
DIRT-CO
DIRT-CO
COOL! IS THIS GOING TO BE ANOTHER STANDOFF LIKE AT THE FREEMAN COMPOUND, DAD?
NO, BOY. EVERYONE IN THAT SITUATION WAS A BULLHEADED NUT-JOB!
I'M RUNNING THIS SHOW!
DAD, YOU CAN'T WIN THIS. WE SIMPSONS HAVE NEVER WITHSTOOD AN ASSAULT BY ORGAN-IZED FORCES!
REMEMBER WHEN THE GIDEONS BLEW UP OUR CAR TO GET BACK THOSE BIBLES YOU STOLE?
PLEASE HOMIE, END THIS THING. YOU DID TAKE THEIR POOL.
OH, YES, HOMIE! DO WHAT THE LITTLE WOMAN TELLS YOU, OR NO SUPPER TONIGHT!
EXCUSE ME! DON'T YOU KNOW IT'S RUDE TO EAVES-DROP ON A FAMILY DISCUSSION??
LOOK WHO'S TALKING--A WALKING BLUE HIBISCUS BUSH! HAW!
HEY! CUT IT OUT!
YEAH? WHO'S GOING TO MAKE US, LITTLE GIRL?
WE ARE!

YOU BOYS MESSED WITH THE WRONG POOL PARTY!
I'M READY TO KICK SOME CONSTRUCTION WORKER BUTT! IT'S BEEN A WHILE.
WE'RE WITH YOU, HOMER!
SPRINGSTEEN! SPRINGSTEEN!
YEAH!
NO ONE INSULTS OUR GOOD FRIEND MADGE!
IN THAT CASE...STEP UP AND BE COUNTED!
THE RESOURCES OF HERMAN'S MILITARY SURPLUS ARE AT YOUR DISPOSAL!
SOON...
SO HE WANTS TO PLAY HARD-BALL, EH?
THEN HARDBALL IT IS!
SAY! WHAT'S ALL THE COMMOTION HERE? JEEZ, YOU LEAVE FOR A COUPLE HOURS AND ALL HECK BREAKS LOOSE.
THE IDIOT WHO LIVES HERE WON'T GIVE UP HIS ILLEGAL SWIMMING POOL. HE'S TURNED THE WHOLE PLACE INTO A COMPOUND.
GOOD LORD! MY SON'S IN THERE!
AND HIS CHICKEN'S OUT HERE!

WAAAAH! I WANT TO GO, I DON'T WANNA STAY!
DON'T BE FOOLISH, SON! YOU CAN'T MAKE IT OVER THE FENCE! JUST LOOK AT THE LAST POOR SOUL WHO TRIED.
OH, GREAT! NOW I'VE GOT AN ITCH!
... FORTY-SEVEN, FORTY EIGHT. IF WE ALL CONSERVE JUST A LITTLE, WE SHOULD BE ABLE TO HOLD OUT FOR A FEW DAYS.
MAAARRRGE!
DO WE HAVE ANY MORE CANS OF SWEDISH MEATBALLS IN HEAVY GRAVY? THEY ARE DELISH!
HRRRRRMM!
THEY THINK THEY'RE SO TOUGH, PRANCING AROUND AFTER A STOLEN AFTERNOON SWIM. LET'S SEE HOW THEY LIKE THINGS WITHOUT ELECTRICITY!
BUZZ-ZAP!
YOU LIKE APPLES, SIMPSON? WELL, HOW DO YA LIKE THEM APPLES?
YOU'VE GOT APPLES?

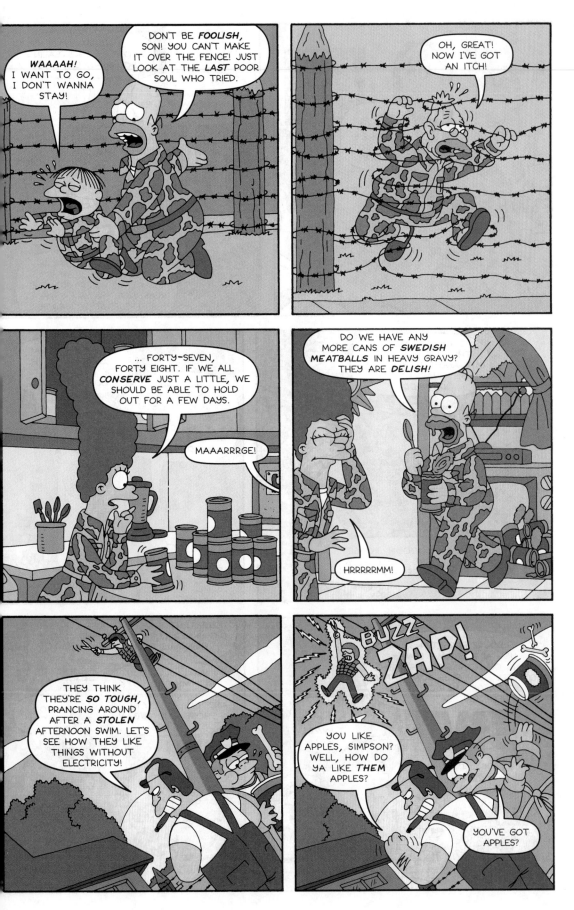

WHAT TH...SOME-HOW HE'S STILL GOT POWER!
I MIGHT HAVE KNOWN! HE'S STEALING YOUR POWER, TOO!
ARE YOU SURE IT'S A GOOD IDEA TO TAKE AWAY THEIR ELECTRICITY?
THIS IS PSYCHOLOGICAL WARFARE, MR. FLANDERS, MEANT TO WEED-OUT THE WEAKLINGS. I WONDER WHO'LL BE THE FIRST TO CRACK?
AAAAAAAH! THE TV'S BLACKED-OUT AND THE BEER WILL GET WARM! WE'RE DOOMED!!
OOOOOH, FORGET IT! WE MIGHT AS WELL SURRENDER NOW!
GEE, DAD. YOU'RE NOT GIVING UP ARE YOU? YOU ALWAYS SAID THE ONLY FIGHTS WORTH WINNING WERE THE HARD FIGHTS.
ACTUALLY, I WAS JUST READING THE SIDE OF A WHEATIES BOX OUT LOUD.
YOU'RE FORGETTING, YOU ADULTS HAVE SOME-THING ON YOUR SIDE THAT THE CONSTRUCTION GUYS DON'T--THE YOUTH OF AMERICA! WE'LL HELP YOU BEAT THEM!
I'LL BE THE CAMP TUNNEL RAT!
EXCELLENT IDEA, MILHOUSE. DIG UNDER ENEMY LINES AND BRING US BACK SOME SUPPLIES.
MAKE SURE YOU GET MY DAD LOTS OF ICE FOR HIS BEER... AND I'LL HAVE ONE OF THOSE FINE CUBAN CIGARS!
YOU GOT IT!

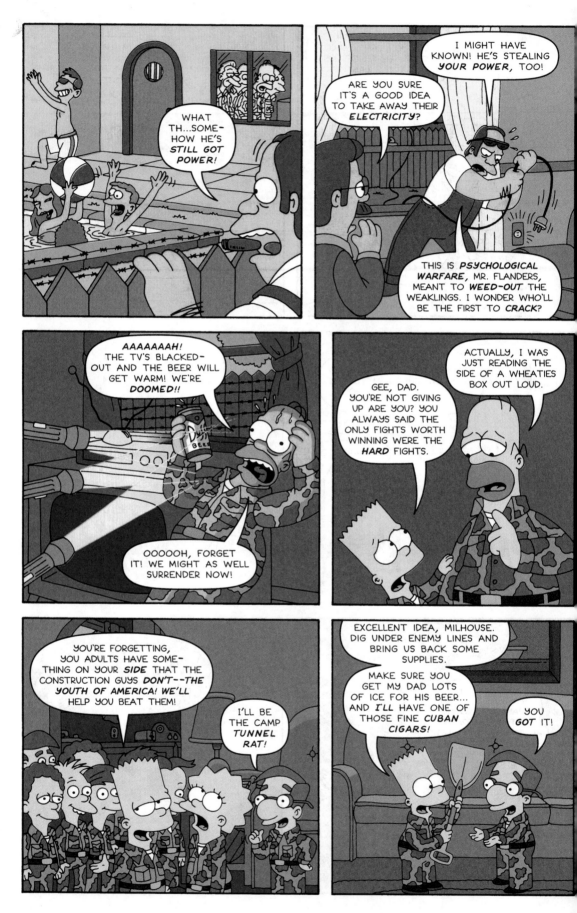

WOW! IF THE KIDS ARE WILLING TO HELP, CAN WE DO ANY LESS?
WAY TO GO, SMALL FRIES! WE'RE WITH YOU!
ENCORE, BOSS! ENCORE!
GOSH, BART! I NEVER KNEW YOU COULD BE SO PERSUASIVE.
GOTTA BE, LIS. THE LONGER THIS GOES ON, THE LONGER WE GET TO DITCH SCHOOL!
AS LONG AS THE ADULTS DON'T GO STIR CRAZY, IT SHOULD BE SMOOTH SAILING.
WELCOME TO THE LENNY AND CARL SHOW! I'M LENNY AND HE'S CARL.
ON TODAY'S SHOW: DEALING WITH A SMELLY CO-WORKER.
THE TV'S BACK ON!
OOOH! HIGH DEFINITION!
COMES THE DAWN...
THE WAY I FIGURE IT, MILHOUSE IS JUST ON THE OTHER SIDE OF THE LINE OF TRUCKS BY NOW.
HE'D BETTER BRING ME THE MAGAZINES I ASKED FOR.
OH, NO! THEY'RE PLAYING MUSIC AT FULL VOLUME!
...'80'S POP...MUSIC!
AAAAAAAAH!!
...YOU'RE TOO SHY, SHY...HUSH, HUSH...
LET'S SEE HOW LONG THEY CAN TAKE THIS!

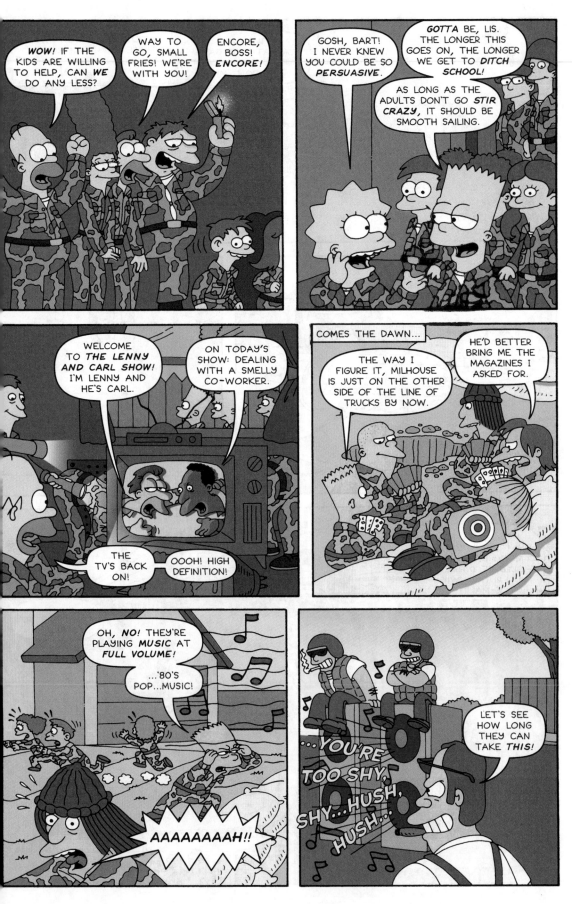

TWO CAN PLAY AT THIS GAME! UNFURL THE SECRET WEAPON, MEN!
GRRRR! BITING 19TH CENTURY POLITICAL CARTOONING! THESE GUYS PLAY ROUGH!
"You'd best bring life preservers when you swim with the pool sharks!"
THEY CAN'T GET AWAY WITH THAT! LET'S SCRATCH CHALKBOARDS! LET'S MOON THEM! LET'S FLING BRASSIERES AT THEM AS IF THEY WERE ELVIS!
NO, WAIT, I GOT IT! LET'S THROW ROCKS!
SPROING!
ACCORDING TO MY TRUSTY JUNIOR CAMPER COMPASS, I SHOULD BE DIRECTLY UNDER THE KWIK-E-MART!
THWACK!
OH, NO! BUCK, ARE YOU OKAY??
WORLD'S STRONGEST MAGNET
HOFFA
I LIKE IKE!

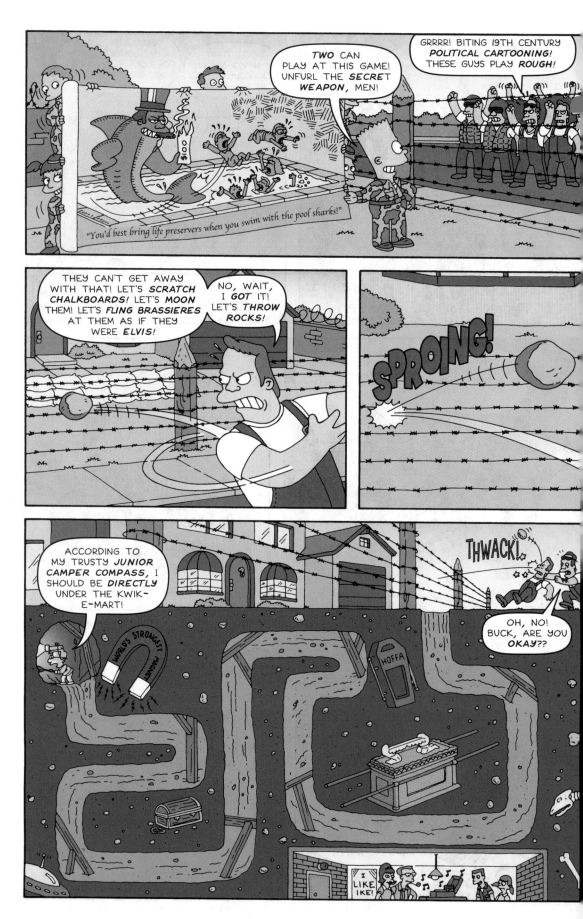

DAMN YOU, SIMPSON! YOU'VE LEFT ME **NO CHOICE**!
IT'S TIME TO CALL IN THE SPRINGFIELD POOL BUILDERS AND FAST-FOOD FRY-COOKS UNION **MILITIA**!
AH, COULD YOU HAVE THEM STOP BY LARD LAD'S AND PICK UP A COUPLE DOZEN DONUTS ON THE WAY?
THE UNION MILITIA? BUT **NOBODY'S** EVER CALLED **THEM** OUT BEFORE!
NOBODY EVEN KNOWS HOW TO GET **IN TOUCH** WITH THEM!
DON'T WORRY, BOYS. THE MILITIA'S LIKE **THE A-TEAM**! THEY ALWAYS SHOW UP WHEN YOU **REALLY** NEED THEM.
WELL...WE REALLY NEED THEM **NOW**!
WELL, LUCKY US! THEY'RE RIGHT OVER THERE!
HEY! WHATCHOO LOOKIN' AT??
AND, SO...
HUT HUT HUT HUT HUT!!
SCREEEEECH!
SLAMM!

STAY AWAY FROM THE EXPLODING SHELLS, RALPHIE, HONEY.
WE HAVEN'T A CHANCE AGAINST THIS KIND OF FIRE-POWER.
TIME TO PULL OUT THE WHITE FLAG.
THERE'S NO SHAME IN AN HONORABLE SURRENDER...HOWEVER, I DID BRING HARI KARI KNIVES IF ANYONE FEELS LED...
GIVE UP? I DON'T KNOW THE MEANING OF THE WORD!
WHATEVER! WE'VE COME TOO FAR! ARE WE NOT MEN... PLUS SOME DARN STRONG WOMEN AND A BUNCH OF SISSY KIDS?
THAT'S TWO WORDS, DAD.
CRASH!
HEY!
YOU ALL KNOW WHAT TO DO.
FREE AT LAST!
AW, NUTS!
WHEW! THAT'S A LOT OF WORK!
WHOEVER SAYS STEVE MCQUEEN WASN'T A MAN'S MAN, IS JUST PLAIN CRAZY.
RRRRRRUMBLE!
CRUMMMMBLE!
WHUH-OH!

I WARNED YOU, SIMPSON! NOBODY STEALS FROM THE POOL GUY! NOW, STEP ASIDE!
NEVER!
HAVE IT YOUR WAY. FORWARD, MEN!
CHUGGA-CHUGGA-CHUGGA!
CHUGGA-CHUGGA!
CHUGGA-CHUGGA!
CHUGGA-CHUGGA!
CHUGGA!

WAIT A MINUTE! WAIT, STOP!
I CAN'T DO IT. I CAN'T RISK KILLING AN ENTIRE FAMILY OVER ONE LOUSY POOL--EVEN IF THAT LUNKHEAD DID STEAL IT!
THAT'S MR. LUNKHEAD TO YOU!
I'M GONNA WALK AWAY HERE, BUT IF THERE WAS ANY JUSTICE IN THE WORLD, I'D GET SOME SORT OF PAY-BACK!
DID YOU HEAR THAT, FAMILY? I WON!
WHOO-HOO!
RRUMBLE!
HMMM... THAT WAS ODD.
CRUNCH!
CRACK!
CRRRACKK!
HRRRRRM! I CAN'T SAY I LIKE THE LOOKS OF THIS!
RRRRUMBLE!
THOOM!!

HMM...A **SINK HOLE,** PROBABLY CAUSED BY **UNDERGROUND TUNNELING**.
NOW **THAT'S** SOME MIGHTY FINE **PAYBACK!**
SSSSSSSSSSS
COME ON, MEN. LET'S GO HOME.
HEY, SIMPSON! I'VE GOT THE NUMBER OF A **GOOD CARPENTER** IF YOU NEED IT!
LATER...
SO LONG, DEAR. WE'LL BE STAYING WITH MY SISTERS UNTIL YOU GET THE MESS CLEANED UP.
WATCH OUT FOR **QUICKSAND,** HOMER!
YEAH, YEAH!
SOD
MY, MY! THAT'S QUITE A **DISASTER AREA** YOU'VE GOT THERE, NEIGHBOR! MIGHT WANT TO CHECK THE **SEWER LINES,** I THINK I SMELL **PEE**-DIDDILY-**YEW!**
SHUT UP, FLANDERS!
STUPID FLANDERS... **STUPID** POOL GUY... **STUPID** HOT WEATHER... **STUPID** COLLAPSED TUNNELS...**STUPID** MUD...**STUPID** PEE-DIDDLY-YEW...
SOD
H-HELLO? IS **ANYBODY** THERE? IS THE SIEGE OVER? I'D LIKE TO COME OUT NOW!
THE END

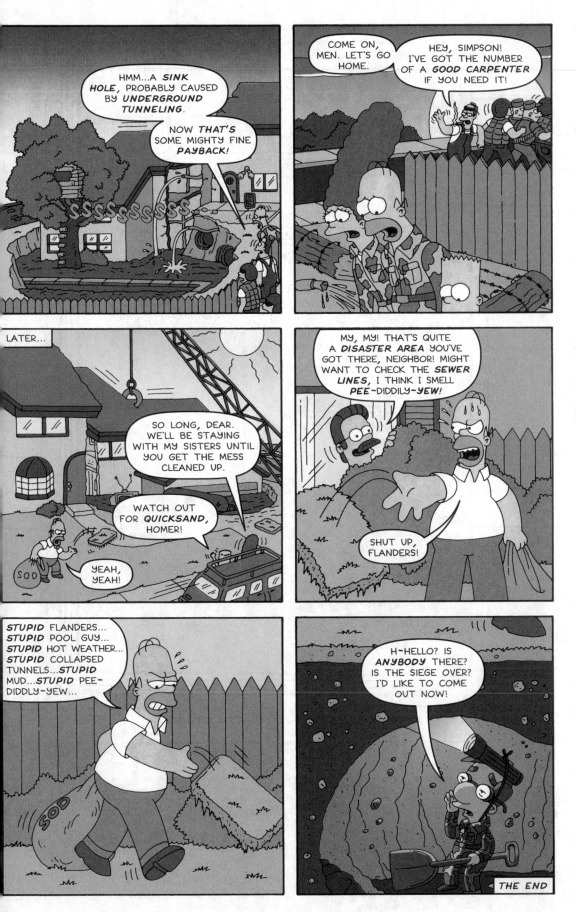

IT'S A DUFF, DUFF, DUFF, DUFF, DUFF WORLD
MATT GROENING
SCOTT SHAW!
Barrington

"Duff Daddy!"
WRITTEN & DRAWN BY: SCOTT SHAW!
INKED BY: TIM BAVINGTON
COLORED BY: CHRIS UNGAR
LETTERED BY: KAREN BATES
EDITED BY: BILL MORRISON
BROUGHT TO YOU BY OUR PROUD SPONSOR: MATT GROENING
OKAY, PEOPLE, SMOAKE & MEERERS HAS GOTTA COME UP WITH A FRESH, NEW AD CAMPAIGN FOR THE DUFF BEER ACCOUNT!
MADISON AVE.
SO, ANY SUGGESTIONS, PEOPLE?
MAYBE IF WE INFERRED THAT NOT DRINKING DUFF BEER CAUSED DANDRUFF?
SALES
I DON'T THINK SO... AFTER ALL, HONESTY IS WHAT THE ADVERTISING BUSINESS IS ALL ABOUT!
WE NEED TO APPEAL TO THE 20 PER CENT OF BEER BUYERS WHO ACCOUNT FOR OVER 80 PER CENT OF ALL BEER SALES...
OR AS THE AGENCY LIKES TO CALL THEM, "HEAVY USERS"!
OR AS I LIKE TO CALL 'EM, "ALCOHOLICS"!
WE NEED THE OL' "SLICE-OF-LIFE" APPROACH! SOMETHING THAT THE "JOE AVERAGE" BEER DRINKER CAN RELATE TO!
ARE YOU KIDDING? BEER DRINKERS RELATE ONLY TO BIG BOOBS AND TALKING ANIMALS!
THAT'S IT! WE'LL CONDUCT A GRASSROOTS TALENT SEARCH TO FIND TWO "TYPICAL" DUFF DRINKERS.
ONE WHO'S A BIG BOOB!
AND ANOTHER ONE WHO LOOKS AND ACTS LIKE A TALKING ANIMAL!
AND WE'LL PIT ONE AGAINST THE OTHER, TRYING TO STEAL THE DUFF BEER! AFTER ALL, OUR FOCUS GROUP RESEARCH TELLS US THAT IF SOMETHING'S GOOD ENOUGH TO STEAL, IT MUST BE GOOD!
SO WHY ISN'T THE AGENCY APPLYING THAT THEORY TO OUR CAR COMMERCIALS?
GOOD WORK, PEOPLE! I THINK SMOAKE & MEERERS HAS ANOTHER BIG HIT ON ITS CORPORATE HANDS!

AND SO, A SCANT SEVEN WEEKS LATER...
Y'KNOW, THERE'S NOTHIN' LIKE SPENDING SOME QUALITY TIME WITH MY FAVORITE BEVERAGE-OF-CHOICE, DUFF BEER!
MMM, DUFF-Y!
HEY, WATCH ME TRICK FRED, ER, I MEAN, HOMER OUTTA HIS DUFF BEER!
G'DAY, MATE! CRIKEY! LET'S THROW A CROC ON THE BARBIE! GORGEOUS, EH WOT?
WHO THE HELL ARE YOU SUPPOSED TO BE, BARNEY?
I'M THAT AUSTRALIAN CROC-HUNTIN' GUY FROM CABLE TELEVISION!
I'LL SAY YOU'RE A CROCK! JUST STAY AWAY FROM MY DUFF BEER!
OH, YOU MEAN THIS DUFF BEER? THE ONE THAT LOOKS DELIGHTFULLY ICE-COLD, INVITINGLY THIRST-QUENCHING?
DUFF
BEER
THE ONE THAT'S PRACTICALLY CALLING OUT MY NAME? THIS ONE, PERHAPS?
GLUG-GLUG-GLUG-GLUG!
YEAH, FRED, I GUESS THAT WOULD BE THE ONE, ALL RIGHT...
BARNEY, WHY ARE YOU CALLING ME "FRED"? HOW WOULD YOU LIKE IT IF I STARTED CALLING YOU "OTIS"?
POP!
SSSSSSSS
SHEESH! HOW DEFLATING! GUESS IT'S TIME TO GO BACK TO THE DRAWING BOARD!

Y'KNOW, IT OCCURS TO ME THAT ALL THESE DISGUISES AND GADGETS PROBABLY COST A LOT MORE THAN IF I JUST WENT TO THE LIQUOR STORE AND BOUGHT A CASE OR TWO OF DUFF BEER...
--NAHHH!
HEY-HEY-HEY!!! HOOOWAHAHA!!! I'M KRUSTY!
OKAY, TELL ME, BOY, IS THIS GUY THE REAL DEAL!?
NO WAY, HOMER! I GIVE THIS CLOWN TWO BIG THUMBS DOWN!
HEY, YOU HEARD IT FROM AN EXPERT, FELLA! SHOVE OFF!
JEEPERS, MISTER, HARVESTING MUSH-ROOMS CAN BE AWFUL THIRSTY WORK!
SO IS GETTING RID OF POINTY-EARED BEER-MOOCHERS! BEAT IT!
:SIGH!: GEE, SCRATCHY, IF ONLY I COULD GET MY PAWS ON THAT DUFF BEER!
I KNOW, ITCHY--YOU COULD BREAK THE BOTTLE AND USE IT TO REPEATEDLY STAB ME! (TO SURREALLY COMEDIC EFFECT, OF COURSE!)
SORRY, BARNEY, NOT EVEN IF YOU HAD A "POOCHIE" PUPPET.
I PITY THE FOOL WHO DOESN'T SHARE HIS DUFF!
SORRY, BARNEY, BUT YOU'RE NOT EXACTLY A-TEAM MATERIAL!
HEY, FRED! BETTY SENT ME OVER TO "BORROW" SOME OF YOUR DUFF BEER! :HYEH-HYEH-HYEH!:
BARNEY, I ALREADY TOLD YOU, STOP CALLING ME "FRED"! BEAT IT!

ALL RIGHT, BARNEY, WHAT ARE YOU SUPPOSED TO BE THIS TIME? A CARPENTER?
NOPE.
A DOWN-ON-HIS-LUCK SURFER?
GUESS AGAIN.
--A CATERER FOR AN EXCLUSIVE TERMITE COLONY?
SORRY.
--THEN, WHAT?!?
I GUESS YOU COULD CALL ME--
WUGHHH...
KLOP!
--"THE CHAIRMAN OF THE BOARD!" CHUCKLE!
OHHHH...
DUFF AND DUFF LITE BEER, A POWERFUL PART OF THIS "HEAVY USER'S" GOOD BREAKFAST!
Duff
DUFF BRAU
UMM, EXACTLY HOW MUCH DID THEY PAY YOU TO BE IN THAT COMMERCIAL, HOMIE?
HEY, I'M NO DUMMY! I GOT THIRTY-SEVEN CASES OF DUFF BEER! AND I FINESSED 'EM INTO THROWIN' IN A 40-POUND BAG OF BEER NUTS!
THAT WAS THE LONGEST 30-SECOND TV COMMERCIAL I'VE EVER SEEN!
GOOD THING I BROUGHT A BOOK!
WOW, HOMER, YOU WERE GREAT! YOUR PERFORMANCE OUGHTTA WIN AN ADVERTISING AWARD IN THE CATEGORY OF "BEST PERFORMANCE BY A BIG BOOB"!
MMM, DUFF... WATCH ME TRICK HOMER...!
HEY, THAT'S ADVERTISING!

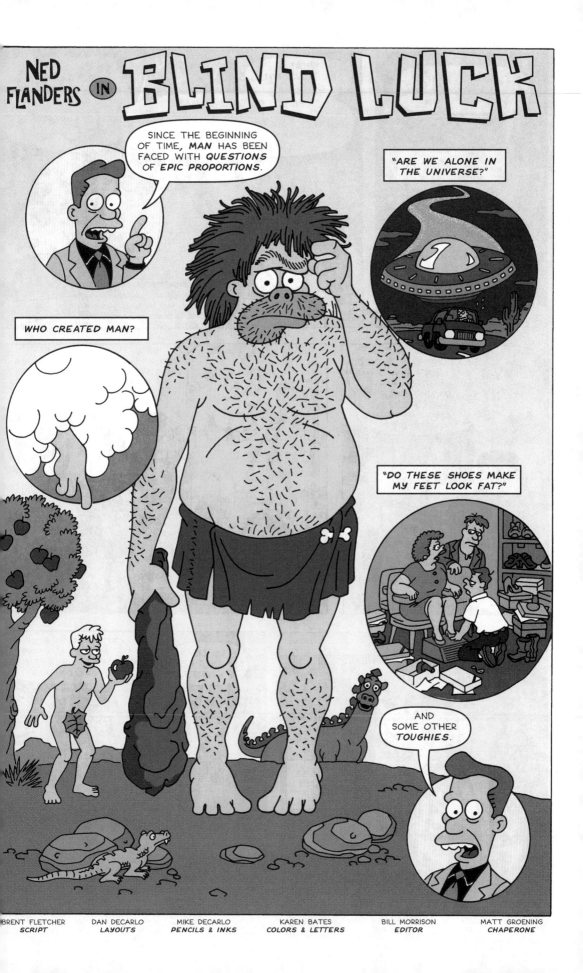

NED FLANDERS IN BLIND LUCK

SINCE THE BEGINNING OF TIME, *MAN* HAS BEEN FACED WITH *QUESTIONS* OF *EPIC PROPORTIONS*.

"ARE WE ALONE IN THE UNIVERSE?"

WHO CREATED MAN?

"DO THESE SHOES MAKE MY FEET LOOK FAT?"

AND SOME OTHER *TOUGHIES*.

BRENT FLETCHER
SCRIPT

DAN DECARLO
LAYOUTS

MIKE DECARLO
PENCILS & INKS

KAREN BATES
COLORS & LETTERS

BILL MORRISON
EDITOR

MATT GROENING
CHAPERONE

TONIGHT, WE TRY TO ANSWER ONE SUCH QUESTION...
WHAT'S THE DEAL WITH CHICKS!?!
HELLO, I'M CHAZ D'AMATO AND TONIGHT ON BLIND LUCK ONE MAN WILL TRY TO ANSWER THIS QUESTION AND MAYBE DISCOVER VICTORIA'S SECRET ALONG THE WAY!
BLIND LUCK
DISCLAIMER: NO BLIND PEOPLE WERE HURT IN THE MAKING OF THIS PROGRAM.
OUR FIRST CONTESTANT IS NED FLANDERS! NED HAS RECENTLY STARTED DATING SINCE HIS MARRIAGE FELL APART AFTER HIS WIFE DIED.
SINS AND SENSIBILITY
BAPTISTS VS. EPISCOPALIANS: WHO THROWS BETTER PARTIES?
CATHOLIC KUNG-F LAYING THE UN-CHASTE TO WASTE
HIS DATE IS JASMINE DOVER. JASMINE IS HOME SCHOOLED AND BY HOME SHE MEANS THE STREETS. SHE PRIDES HERSELF ON NEVER GETTING PREGNANT AND STILL HAVING ALL TEN FINGERS.
TRAS
"LET THE FIREWORKS BEGIN!"
HI DIDDLY HO...
2C
MY DOG DOESN'T BITE...
...BUT I DO.
NED SAYS HE DOESN'T LIKE SURPRISES.
...LY COW! MY EYES FEEL SO DIRTY.
DON'T WORRY, HON'. I'VE GOT SOME VISINE FOR THAT. I BUY IT BY THE GALLON JUG.
SURPRISE!

SO, UH, JASMINE, WHAT DO YOU DO FOR A LIVING?
RIGHT NOW I'M WORKING AT TRY-N-SAVE. I'M TRYING TO SKIM ENOUGH MONEY FROM THE REGISTERS TO BUY A USED MICROWAVE.
RICK'S RIFLE RANGE
ALRIGHTY, DATERINO. THE FIRST THING THEY'VE GOT US DOING IS A LITTLE SKEET SHOOTING. HAVE YOU EVER SHOT A GUN BEFORE?
SURE. I SHOOT AT MY NEIGHBOR'S DOGS ALL THE TIME. I'M LOOKIN' TO MAKE ME A FUR COAT.
ENDORSED BY: CHARLTON HESTON OF THE NRA AND ALLEN IVERSON OF THE NBA
KNIFE THROWING
BEGINNERS
EXPERTS
NUGENTS
JUST LIKE AN EPISODE OF "THE A-TEAM."
THIS SEEMS LIKE GOOD, CLEAN FUN. IT'S A LITTLE VIOLENT, BUT WITHOUT ANY BLOODSHED.
MR. T SAYS, "I PITY THE FOOL ON THIS DATE!"
WELL I'LL BE A RIPE TURNIP! I SHOT THREE OUT OF FIVE!
YOU'RE A REGULAR ANNIE OAKLEY. NOW MOVE OVER TWINKLE TOES.
NUGENTS
MY, YOU SEEM AWFUL HANDY WITH THAT SHOTGUN.
I JUST CLOSE MY EYES AND LISTEN TO THE VOICES IN MY HEAD.
SO DID THE SON OF SAM, TED BUNDY, AND CHARLIE MANSON.

YOU KNOW, ACCORDING TO THIS DATING BOOK, YOU SHOULD BE IN THE FRONT SEAT WITH ME!
WELL, I USUALLY END UP IN THE BACK SEAT, SO I THOUGHT I'D SAVE SOME TIME!
DATING GUIDE
The GILDED TRUFFLE
GUESS YOUR VALET'S BLOOD ALCOHOL LEVEL, WIN A FREE CAR DEODORIZER.
THIS PLACE LOOKS FANCY. HOLD ON WHILE I CHANGE INTO SOMETHING A LITTLE MORE APPROPRIATE.
THIS PLACE HAS CLASS. KENNY ROGERS-TYPE CLASS. EVERYONE IS WEARING SHIRTS AND THE SILVERWARE AIN'T EVEN PLASTIC.
JASMINE TOLD BLIND LUCK SHE HAS EIGHT TATTOOS. WE CAN ONLY SEE TWO.
WHY DID WE HAVE TO STOP AT EVERY TABLE?
I WANTED THE PERFECT TABLE TO MAKE THIS THE MOST ROMANTIC EVENING EVER.
COULD WE GET SOME SILVERWARE HERE?
OUR SPECIAL TONIGHT IS A ROASTED DUCK LIGHTLY MARINATED IN VINAIGRETTE AND GARNISHED WITH BELGIAN CAPERS.
THAT SOUNDS GREAT. GO AHEAD AND SUPER-SIZE MINE.
THAT'S SIX GLASSES OF WINE. MAYBE YOU OUGHT TO SLOW DOWN A LITTLE.
SO YOU WANT TO ARM-WRESTLE?
NED SAYS HE'S NOT AFRAID TO TAKE AN OCCASIONAL RISK. ONCE A YEAR HE EATS THAI BBQ.
Velvet Blasphemy
LIVE DANCIN
MOPING
NOW IT'S TIME FOR A LITTLE DANCING. WE SHOULDN'T HAVE TO WORRY ABOUT THIS VIOLATING YOUR PAROLE.
PAROLE SURE CAN BE TOUGH. THERE ARE DAYS I FEEL LIKE I CAN'T BE WITHIN FIVE-HUNDRED YARDS OF ANYONE!

I FEEL LIKE I'M IN A WHERE'S WALDO BOOK WRITTEN BY THE DEVIL.
THAT SOUNDS LIKE A GOOD BOOK FOR MY NIECE.
EXIT
LET'S SEE IF NED CAN DANCE THE FRIGHT AWAY.
WHAT DO THESE PEOPLE DO DURING THE DAY?
MOST OF THEM WORK AT **HALLMARK**.
OH NO, MY EX-HUSBAND ANTON IS HERE. AND HE'S FOAMING AT THE MOUTH AGAIN.
HOW LONG HAVE YOU TWO BEEN ***DIVORCED***?
WELL THE DIVORCE ISN'T ***OFFICIALLY LEGAL***. BUT I DID WRITE DOWN THE PHRASE "CATCH YOU LATER" ON A NAPKIN.
AAAGGHHH!!!
PLAYING HARD TO GET, NED? THAT ***TURNS ME ON***!
BLIND LUCK
WELL, IT LOOKS LIKE THAT WAS ***NOT*** A MATCH MEANT TO BE. MAYBE NED'S GAY. BUT IS IT THE LAST TIME HE'LL EVER SEE JASMINE?
WELL, WHEN JASMINE THREATENED ONE OF OUR PRODUCERS, HE ***GLADLY*** GAVE HER ***NED'S ADDRESS AND PHONE NUMBER***. SO GOOD NIGHT AMERICA AND ***GOOD LUCK, NED!***
THE END?

SIMPSONS
COMICS
BONGO COMICS GROUP
#56
US $2.50
CAN $3.50
APPROVED BY THE COMICS CODE AUTHORITY

DON'T MOVE A MUSCLE. DON'T EVEN BLINK. ALL RIGHT, TIME TO LET YOU HAVE IT...
THE YES-MAN WHO WOULD BE King

THE YES-MAN WHO WOULD BE King

DOUG TUBER, TIM MAILE, STEVE LUCHSINGER *SCRIPT* · JOHN COSTANZA *PENCILS* · TIM BAVINGTON *INKS* · ART VILLANUEVA *COLORS* · KAREN BATES *LETTERS* · BILL MORRISON *EDITOR* · MATT GROENING *MONARCH OF MIRTH*

I'LL WING MY TOPPER ONTO YOUR LEFT, OR SINISTER, HAND, SNATCH MY OPERA HAT, AND BE OFF TO THE THEATER!
OOF!
EXCELLENT TOSS, SIR. I COULD TELL YOU WERE AIMING FOR THAT FLOOR TILE.
PLOP!
MY AIM WAS PUT OFF BY THE RAZOR-SHARP STEEL I HAD INSERTED IN THE BRIM. WEIGHS ME DOWN, BUT IT'LL MAKE A DANDY SURPRISE FOR THE NEXT ROUGHNECK LOOKING TO WAYLAY ME.
WELL DONE, SMITHERS. YOU MAKE A FINE SUBSTITUTE HAT RACK.
WHEN WILL YOUR ELEPHANT-IVORY HAT-RACK COME BACK FROM THE POLISHER'S, SIR?
TOMORROW. SO I'LL NEED YOU TO STAND HERE ALL NIGHT. AND DON'T MOVE--I DON'T LIKE IT WHEN HAT RACKS MOVE, UNLESS THEY'RE FEATURED IN A MUSICAL NUMBER IN A JOLLY CARTOON.
I'LL BE HERE, SIR. NOT MOVING.

BUT A HAT RACK CAN ALWAYS **DREAM**...
RING RING
"SMITHERS! WHERE ARE YOU?"
HUH?
SMITHERS, COME HERE! I **NEED YOU**!
RING RING
IT'S MORNING! I MUST HAVE DOZED OFF!
I'M HERE, SIR. DON'T UPSET YOURSELF. YOU'RE PRONE TO **VAPORS**!
RING
I COULDN'T SLEEP LAST NIGHT, SO I WATCHED "THE MAKING OF 'I'LL TAKE SWEDEN.'" THAT ANITA EKBERG IS QUITE A **DISH**. CONSEQUENTLY, I HAVE A YEN FOR **SWEDISH FOOD**. SCAMPER DOWN TO **LITTLE STOCKHOLM** AND FETCH ME SOME ROLLMOPS, HERRING-MIT-BROD AND AQUAVIT.
I'LL BE BACK BEFORE YOU CAN SAY "KALHYGGEN OCH FORBRANNING," SIR!

SOON, IN THE SECTION OF SPRINGFIELD KNOWN AS *LITTLE STOCKHOLM*...
VOLVO REPAIR and Sauna
SKOLL! LITTLE STOCKHOLM! SPRINGFIELD'S HIGHEST SUICIDE RATE! PARKING FREE WITH VALIDATION!
VOLVO
HELD OVER 1,807TH WEEK SCENES FROM A MARRIAGE
Stewardess School and Sauna
SMORGASBORD and SAUNA
HMMM, I HAVE THE **FLATBROD** AND THE **AQUAVIT**. CAN'T FIND THE **GRAVLAX**...
STOCK UP ON STOCKHOLM STOCKINGS
MAX VON SYDOW NUTCRACKERS
DEATH TO DANDRUFF Shampoo
CAN I HELP YOU FIND SOMETHING?
I CAN'T FIND GRAVLAX. HOW CAN THERE BE **MEANING IN LIFE**?
THERE IS NO MEANING. ALL LIFE IS AN **AGONY** OF WINTER WINDS AND **SORROW**. BUT SMOKED FISH IS ON AISLE THREE.
GASP!
BY THE BEARD OF CRAFTY ODIN, FATHER GOD OF NEIGHBORING NORWAY...
...THE RESEMBLANCE IS UNCANNY!
OPERATOR, GET ME NORSE-SIDE 777.
HELLO, **SWEDISH EMBASSY**?

...AND A HERRING-AND-WATERCRESS SALAD WHICH TOOK ME TWO HOURS TO MAKE.
I'VE CHANGED MY MIND. I WANT SOMETHING MORE ROBUST FOR BREAKFAST. STEAK AND EGGS SHOULD BE JUST WHAT THE DOCTOR ORDERED.
OF COURSE, I'LL NEED YOU TO CHEW IT UP AND REGURGITATE IT FOR ME. I'LL WAIT.
DING-♫ ♫ DONG!
CAN I HELP YOU?
OLAV GUSTAVSON, MASTER OF HERALDRY FOR THE ROYAL HOUSE OF SWEDEN.
INGA CARLSDOTTIR, PROFESSOR OF GENEOLOGY, UNIVERSITY OF GOTEBORG.
GRETTA LILLQUIST, DEEP-TISSUE MASSAGE, IN-CALL, OUT-CALL.
MR. SMITHERS, THE CURRENT KING OF SWEDEN IS AT DEATH'S DOOR, MAKING ME SAD.
HEH, HEH. ANOTHER OLD FOE I'VE OUTLIVED!
YOU ARE EXACTLY LIKE THE KING IN BOTH SPIT AND IMAGE!
THE CURRENT KING HAS NO HEIR. IT IS NINETY-NINE PERCENT CERTAIN THAT YOU, WAYLON SMITHERS, ARE THE LAST IN THE ROYAL LINE!
BUT WE MUST MAKE SURE. I'M HERE TO ADMINISTER A BLOOD TEST, FOLLOWED BY A FULL-BODY MASSAGE.
I MIGHT BE THE KING OF SWEDEN?

SOON, ALL OVER TOWN...
...THAT WAYLON SMITHERS MIGHT BE THE REAL KING OF SWEDEN!
WELL, HE WON'T BE PRODUCING ANY HEIRS.
...SO HE'D PROBABLY GET TO LIVE IN A BIG PALACE!
...SERVANTS CATERING TO HIS EVERY WHIM!
...PAINTING DWARVES GOLD AND USING 'EM AS LIFE-SIZED CHESS PIECES!
...INDOOR HORSE-RACING, NAKED TWISTER, DOGS DRESSED LIKE PEOPLE!
...A WHOLE ROOM MADE OF BEEF JERKY. FURNITURE, CARPET, EVERYTHING! AND A LAKE MADE OF BEER AND A STAFF TO ROW YOU AROUND WHILE YOU DRINK!
AND THEY'RE WELL-NIGH SLAVES! IT'S HOW HE DOES WI' EVERYONE. AND IF YA DISAGREE--THEY CLAP YA IN IRONS AN' INTAE THE DUNGEON WI' YE!
PROPERTY SEIZURES! BEATINGS! RANDOM ARRESTS! TORTURE! JUST LIKE HOME.
TODAY I SAW A CLOUD THAT LOOKED LIKE A CHOO-CHOO!
I HEAR WAYLON SMITHERS MIGHT BE THE REAL KING OF SWEDEN!
HEH,HEH. YOU AND YOUR STORIES.

LATER...
FOR HEAVEN'S SAKE, SMITHERS, STOP SPANKING THAT WRETCHED CREATURE AND LISTEN TO ME. YOU MUST ACT IN A MANNER THAT BEFITS YOUR ROYAL LINEAGE!
WHACK! WHACK!
BUT IT'S AWFULLY DUSTY, SIR...MR. BURNS? WHY DOES THIS GORILLA LOOK SO FIERCE? I'VE ALWAYS HEARD THEY WERE SUCH GENTLE CREATURES.
YES, THEY ARE. NORMALLY.
WHACK!
BUT EVEN THE MOST DOCILE CREATURE CAN BECOME A MIGHTY FORCE UNDER THE PROPER CIRCUMSTANCES. THIS IS A LESSON THAT YOU WOULD DO WELL TO LEARN IF YOU ARE TO BE KING.
AS FOR THIS SIMIAN'S ANGRY EXPRESSION, I MERELY STOLE ITS BABY BEFORE I SHOT IT.
LISTEN, SMITHERS. AS YOU KNOW, IT'S LONG BEEN MY DREAM TO HAVE CORDIAL RELATIONS WITH A NATION WHICH MAINTAINS A FUNCTIONAL WHALING PORT...
IT SEEMS TO ME THAT WHILE YOU WAIT FOR YOUR ROYALTY TO BE CONFIRMED, YOU SHOULD LIVE IN MY HOUSE AS AN HONORED GUEST, AS BEFITS A MAN OF YOUR EXALTED STATION.
AND YOUR DAYS OF SERVITUDE ARE OVER. FROM NOW ON, A BATTERY OF SERVANTS WILL ATTEND TO YOU.

MR. BURNS, I WAS TOLD YOU WANT TO SEE ME. I'M SORRY I ACCIDENTALLY RELEASED RADIOACTIVE WASTE INTO THE CITY'S WATER SUPPLY!
GOOD LORD, YOU REALLY DID THAT?
YES, I DI--UM... I MEAN...THAT IS...WHAT DID YOU WANT TO SEE ME ABOUT?
MY NEW ROYAL FRIEND HERE REQUIRES A STAFF OF LACKEYS, BOOTLICKS AND CHURLS. SO, I'VE BEEN THINKING...
SOON...
EXCELLENT! BUT LET'S HAVE THE CHAMBERMAID AND THE WIZARD SWITCH UNIFORMS.
HOMER, I'M NOT SURE PULLING THE KIDS OUT OF SCHOOL SO THEY CAN BE SERVANTS IS THE BEST IDEA.
AND I WOULD AGREE WITH YOU, MARGE, IF IT WASN'T FOR THREE LITTLE WORDS..."SMOR-GAS-BORD!" IF WE LIVE IN SWEDEN WE MAY NOT BE KINGS, BUT WE CAN EAT LIKE THEM!
THERE'S YOUR ROYAL RETINUE, YOUR HIGHNESS. ENJOY!
I WILL! A FELLOW COULD REALLY GET USED TO THE ROYAL TREATMENT...

IN HONOR OF YOUR IMPENDING ROYALITY, I PRESENT YOU WITH A LUDEFISK-FLAVORED SQUISHEE, AT OUR ROYALTY DISCOUNT OF FIVE PERCENT OFF.
HERRING
HERRING
HERRING
HEY, YOU'RE THAT KING GUY! SO YOU GET THE CLEAN STOOL. Y'KNOW, THELMA RITTER ONCE SAT THERE. SWEET-LOOKIN' WOMAN, BUT BOY, COULD SHE PUT IT AWAY.
DON'T SHAKE DOWN THAT ONE, BOYS. HE'S THE KING OF SOMETHING, SOMEWHERE.
IN MY OFFICIAL CAPACITY AS SOON-TO-BE-CROWNED FIGUREHEAD OF SWEDEN, I DECLARE THE SPRINGFIELD GIANT NOVELTY SCISSORS STORE OPEN!
GRAND OPENING
SNIP!
Liberte
Egalite
Malibu Stacia

OCH! AND YE CALL YERSELF A KING! A KING SHOULD STAND SIX FEET TALL AND WEIGH TWENTY STONE. YER NOTHING BUT A SPECTACLE-WEARIN' COUF WITH A SHELF FULL O' MALIBU STACY DOLLS.
AND YOU CERTAINLY DON'T DISPLAY THE SORT OF TEMPERATE, LAW-GIVING WISDOM OF, FOR INSTANCE, A CHUCK HESTON.
NO, UNTIL I SEE SOME CRACKER-JACK PROCLAMATION MAKING AND THE OCCASIONAL HEAVY-HANDED DEATH SENTENCE, I'LL SAVE MY ALLEGIANCE FOR JESSE "THE BODY" VENTURA.
HMMM...I REALLY HAVEN'T PROVED THAT I DESERVE TO BE KING...THERE MUST BE SOMETHING I CAN DO.
I ASKED HER OUT FIRST!
LISTEN, ER, AH, NEWSBOY, I SAW MISS SCISSORS FIRST, AND I'M TAKING HER OUT!
MISS SCISSORS
FELLAS, FELLAS!
MAYBE I CAN SETTLE THIS. I DO HAVE KINGLY WISDOM, AFTER ALL.
WE'LL HAVE MISS SCISSORS STAND INSIDE THIS CIRCLE. THEN YOU EACH GRAB ONE OF HER ARMS, AND WHOEVER PULLS HER OUT GETS TO DATE HER.
MISS SCISSORS
YOU SEE, WHOEVER REALLY CARES ABOUT THIS WOMAN WON'T PULL ON HER ARM, TO AVOID HURTING HER.
HEH,HEH. JUDICIOUS AND A SEXY SPECTACLE.

SOUNDS LIKE A GOOD PLAN TO ME.
SOMEONE SAY 1,2,3-- GO!
1,2,3-- GO!
BINGO! LET THE GOOD TIMES ROLL!
OW!
SORRY. MISS SCISSORS GOES TO MAYOR QUIMBY, WHO OBVIOUSLY HAS **MORE AFFECTION** FOR HER.
SO LET IT BE WRITTEN, SO LET IT BE DONE.
FOR ONCE, I'M PLEASED TO HAVE **CONGENITALLY SWEATY PALMS,** SINCE MY SLIPPERY GRIP HAS GUARANTEED ME A SATURDAY NIGHT OF **ECSTASY**. AND I OWE IT ALL TO HIS MAJESTY, **KING WAYLON**!
THAT'S RIGHT. GIVE IT UP FOR **KING WAYLON**!
HOORAY FOR KING WAYLON!
DISPENSE WISDOM TO US, TOO!
YEAH! GIVE ME A BIG THING OF **JUSTICE!**

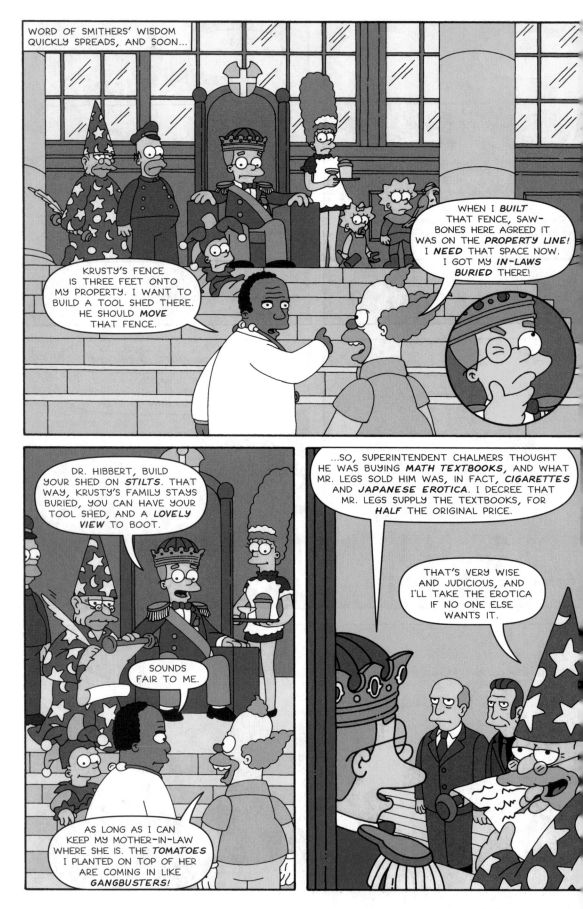

WORD OF SMITHERS' WISDOM QUICKLY SPREADS, AND SOON...

KRUSTY'S FENCE IS THREE FEET ONTO MY PROPERTY. I WANT TO BUILD A TOOL SHED THERE. HE SHOULD *MOVE* THAT FENCE.

WHEN I *BUILT* THAT FENCE, SAW-BONES HERE AGREED IT WAS ON THE *PROPERTY LINE!* I *NEED* THAT SPACE NOW. I GOT MY *IN-LAWS BURIED* THERE!

DR. HIBBERT, BUILD YOUR SHED ON *STILTS.* THAT WAY, KRUSTY'S FAMILY STAYS BURIED, YOU CAN HAVE YOUR TOOL SHED, AND A *LOVELY VIEW* TO BOOT.

SOUNDS FAIR TO ME.

AS LONG AS I CAN KEEP MY MOTHER-IN-LAW WHERE SHE IS. THE *TOMATOES* I PLANTED ON TOP OF HER ARE COMING IN LIKE *GANGBUSTERS!*

...SO, SUPERINTENDENT CHALMERS THOUGHT HE WAS BUYING *MATH TEXTBOOKS,* AND WHAT MR. LEGS SOLD HIM WAS, IN FACT, *CIGARETTES* AND *JAPANESE EROTICA.* I DECREE THAT MR. LEGS SUPPLY THE TEXTBOOKS, FOR *HALF* THE ORIGINAL PRICE.

THAT'S VERY WISE AND JUDICIOUS, AND I'LL TAKE THE EROTICA IF NO ONE ELSE WANTS IT.

MR. SMITHERS IS A GODSEND FROM OUR MANY GODS!
BECAUSE WAYLON SMITHERS DISPLAYS WISDOM AND ASSORTED QUALITIES OF LEADERSHIP UNRELATED TO GRAFT AND WOMANIZING, I HEREBY DEFER ALL CIVIC AUTHORITY TO HIM. ALL HAIL KING WAYLON!
HE'LL TELL US HOW TO LIVE!
HE'S THE BEST THING TO HAPPEN TO THIS TOWN SINCE "CREAMED WEENIE WEDNESDAYS" AT KRUSTY BURGER!
EXCUSE ME, BUT WE SHOULD THINK TWICE BEFORE WE HAND OVER COMPLETE AUTHORITY TO ANY ONE MAN. WE LIVE IN A SYSTEM OF CHECKS AND BALANCES TO PREVENT THE TYRANNY WHICH INEVITABLY FLOWS FROM ABSOLUTE POWER.
GET THE LITTLE GIRL!
SHE'S TRYING TO KEEP US FREE. DESTROY HER!
I LOVE LISA, BUT SHE HAS TO STOP LIVING!
HOLD ON! THIS IS MY LITTLE DAUGHTER! SHE'S PRECIOUS! LET'S JUST TAR AND FEATHER HER AND RUN HER OUT OF TOWN.
HURRY, LISA. HIDE!
THANKS, MOM. I'LL ALWAYS REMEMBER YOU.

AND SO, SMITHERS' WORD WAS LAW THROUGHOUT THE LAND!
WHAT A SHAMEFUL SPECTACLE. A SIGHT LIKE THAT IS A BLOT ON OUR TOWN.
HENCEFORTH, I DECREE THAT ALL BUMS AND BEGGARS BE PROVIDED WITH SMART WARDROBES AND FREE HAIR GROOMING!
HUZZAH!
EXERCISE ISN'T ONLY GOOD FOR YOUNG PEOPLE, IT'S GOOD FOR EVERYONE.
I HEREBY ORDAIN THAT FOR TWO HOURS EVERY AFTERNOON, EACH CITIZEN OF SPRINGFIELD WILL EITHER ROLLER BLADE, ICE DANCE, OR "SWEAT TO THE OLDIES!"
ICE DANCING! HOORAY!
TOMORROW MORNING, AMC IS SHOWING "ALL ABOUT EVE" IN ITS "DAMES WE LOVE" SERIES! I DECLARE THIS A CIVIC HOLIDAY, AND EVERY MAN, WOMAN AND CHILD IS REQUIRED TO SAVOR BETTE DAVIS AND CELESTE HOLME IN THE MOST OUTRAGEOUS CATFIGHT OF THE CENTURY!
HMMM...
I'M ALL FOR CATTY GIRL-FIGHTING ON THE SILVER SCREEN, BUT CLOSING THE SCHOOLS STRIKES ME AS RATHER HIGH-HANDED.
YE CAN SAY THAT AGAIN. WE'RE ONE STEP AWA' FROM RE-EDUCATION CAMPS AND FORCED BREEDIN' BETWEEN STATE-SELECTED COUPLES.
PSST!

LOOK WHAT'S HAPPENING! OUR PRECIOUS FREEDOMS ARE BEING ERODED! SOON WE'LL ALL BE SERFS UNDER THE IRON JACKBOOT OF WAYLON SMITHERS!
WILLIE, WHEN YOU TALK OF FORCED BREEDING BETWEEN STATE-SELECTED COUPLES...CAN ANYONE GET IN ON THAT?
IT'S UP TO US TO FIGHT THIS. WE HAVE TO RECRUIT OTHER FREEDOM-FIGHTERS AND RECLAIM OUR LIBERTY!
WE'RE WI' YOU TA THE DEATH, LASSIE!
IN THE MEANTIME, I PROCLAIM THAT MEN SHALL BE COMFORTABLE DISPLAYING AFFECTION FOR ONE ANOTHER, LIKE THEY DO IN EUROPE.
I LOVE YA, LOU. I'M HERE IF YOU NEED ME.
I DON'T REALLY KNOW YOU, BUT I'M ƸAHEMƷ DELIGHTED TO SEE YOU ƸWOO-HEY!Ʒ!
DUDE!
SOON...
I CALL THIS MEETING OF THE SPRINGFIELD ANTI-MONARCHY LEAGUE TO ORDER.

SPRINGFIELD FREE FOREVER!
CLEARLY, OUR FIRST PRIORITY IS A PLAN OF ACTION TO *ELIMINATE* MR. SMITHERS' TYRANNY. IDEAS?
I THINK WE NEED TO CHANGE OUR *SLOGAN*. THERE'S NO VERB. AS IT'S WRITTEN, "FREE" IS ADJECTIVAL.
I'D LIKE SOMETHING THAT INVOKES THE CREATOR, TO ENSURE DIVINE BENEDICTION ON OUR UPCOMING MAYHEM.
TO *MY* MIND, A LOGO IS NAE A LOGO IF IT DINNA SHOW A ROYAL GETTIN' HIS PONCEY SKULL BATTERED IN WI' A JAGGED ROCK.
I THINK THERE SHOULD BE AN ELEPHANT.
CAN WE FOCUS ON OUR GOAL, PLEASE?
WAIT! WE HAVEN'T HEARD FROM MR. TEENY, YET.
EEEK! YAP! EEEH-EEEH-EEEH!
THANK YOU, MR. TEENY. AS WE KNOW, THE BLOOD TESTS WILL BE IN ON SATURDAY. SMITHERS WILL BE KING OF SWEDEN, AND SPRINGFIELD HAS ALREADY AGREED TO BECOME A *SWEDISH PROTECTORATE*.
SMITHERS' CORONATION PRO-CESSION WILL PASS RIGHT OVER THESE CATACOMBS!

I PROPOSE WE KIDNAP SMITHERS AND SET HIM ADRIFT. HE'LL FLOAT TO SEA, WHERE HE CAN BE TAKEN TO SWEDEN. SPRINGFIELD WILL NEVER LOSE ITS LIBERTY.
SEEMS FINE.
I AGREE WITH THAT.
I VOTE "AYE," WITH THE WEE CHANGE THAT WE USE AN OAR TO BATTER HIS BRAINS INTO PASTE.
NOW, LET'S GET OUT O' HERE-- THIS PLACE HAS A MIGHTY STINK.
IF YOU WANT TO BUY A PAT BOONE CD, THAT'S FINE. YOU DON'T NEED MY PERMISSION.
DANDY!
THAT'S ALL FOR TODAY. THE KING NEEDS HIS REST.
ANYBODY WANNA GO TO LITTLE STOCKHOLM FOR MEATBALLS AND LINGONBERRIES?
I HEAR THEY'VE GOT A PORTRAIT OF KING WAYLON DONE ENTIRELY IN RANUNCULUS.
NAW, I'M GONNA GO WANDER THROUGH THE NEW MUNICIPAL FLOWER GARDEN.

LET'S GET HIS MAJESTY BACK INSIDE.
CAN WE GET YOU ANYTHING? ROYAL SLIPPERS? ROYAL APPLE JUICE? ROYAL CROWN COLA?
NO, THANK YOU. LEAVE ME ALONE, THANK YOU.
IT'S LONELY BEING KING. NO ONE TO CONFIDE IN. NO ONE TO SHARE WITH. NO ONE TO TAKE TO A MIDNIGHT SHOWING OF "HAIRSPRAY."
I DON'T LIKE CHICKEN. SIMPSON, COME HERE.
NO...MORE...CHICKEN! EVER! I WANT CONDOR! CONDOR CUTLETS!
AND THAT SHOULD BE ME GETTING A PERFECTLY GOOD DINNER MASHED IN MY FACE DURING AN INFANTILE TEMPER TANTRUM.
I CAN STAND DISPENSING ROYAL JUSTICE. I CAN SURVIVE LIVING IN WEALTH AND SPLENDID ISOLATION...
BUT I'M GOING TO MISS BEING A SPINELESS LICKSPITTLE TO THAT MAGNIFICENT MAN.

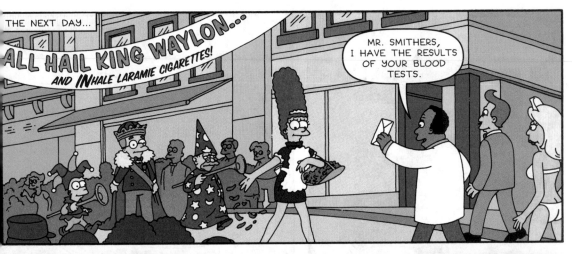

THE NEXT DAY...

ALL HAIL KING WAYLON... AND *IN*HALE LARAMIE CIGARETTES!

MR. SMITHERS, I HAVE THE RESULTS OF YOUR BLOOD TESTS.

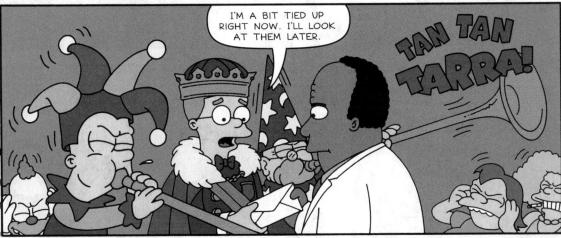

I'M A BIT TIED UP RIGHT NOW. I'LL LOOK AT THEM LATER.

TAN TAN TARRA!

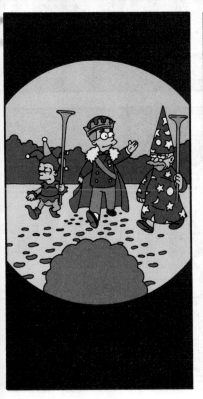

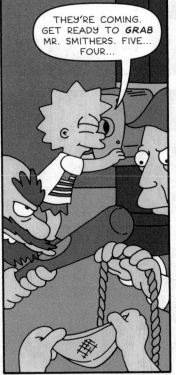

THEY'RE COMING. GET READY TO *GRAB* MR. SMITHERS. FIVE... FOUR...

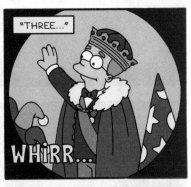

"THREE..."

WHIRR...

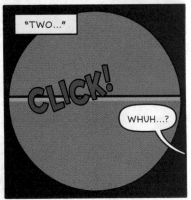

"TWO..."

CLICK!

WHUH...?

THE PERI-SCOPE SHUT OFF! GIMME ANOTHER QUARTER!
I HAVE TWO DIMES AND A NICKEL. IS THAT OKAY?
THERE'S NO TIME! JUST GRAB SMITHERS!
COME TO WILLIE, YA BEAUTY!
WAH! FIRST THE LINDBERGH BABY, NOW ME!
AAH! THAT SUNLIGHT! I'M BLINDED!
NEVERMIND! WE GOT HIM!
KLANK!
IT'S OFF TO THE BRINEY WI' YE NOW, YE POXY RASCAL!
OOF!
WAYLON SMITHERS, DO YOU ACCEPT THE ROLE OF MONARCH, AND ALL PRIVILEGES AND BURDENS THERETO?
NO!
GASP!
HE SAID NO!
SAY IT AIN'T SO!

NOW WE HAVE TO RUN OUR OWN LIVES!
PLEASE, KILL ME! I CAN'T FACE LIFE!
I KNOW YOU ALL THINK I'M A KING. I'VE HEARD THE WHISPERS. I'VE FELT YOUR STARES. BUT I'M NOT A KING. I'M JUST LIKE YOU.
I GET UP IN THE MORNING, HAVE BREAKFAST, AND SEW RHINESTONE OUTFITS FOR MY MALIBU STACY DOLLS.
I READ THE TEST RESULTS, MR. BURNS. I'M NOT THE KING OF SWEDEN. I'M JUST A HUMBLE MAN WHO WANTS NOTHING MORE THAN TO RUB SOOTHING EMOLLIENTS ON YOUR BEDSORES.
VERY WELL, SMITHERS. MY PLANS FOR THE WHALES CAN WAIT. BUT ONE DAY, I WILL SUCCEED. OH, YES-- THE WHALES WILL TASTE MY WRATH.
WELL, MARGE, YOUR "LET'S-ALL-GO-TO-SWEDEN-FOR-FREE" SCHEME BLEW UP IN YOUR FACE. NOW THERE'S NO SMORGAS-BORD FOR ANYONE. WE ALL LOSE!
I DON'T UNDER-STAND. HIS BLOOD TESTS WERE POSITIVE. HE IS THE HEIR TO THE THRONE OF SWEDEN.
BUT THE CURRENT KING DIED THIS MORNING. SWEDEN IS A SHIP WITHOUT A RUDDER.
WELL, IT'S THE 21ST CENTURY. I'M SURE SWEDEN CAN GET ALONG JUST FINE WITHOUT A KING. AHEE, HEE, HEE!

SHØP
SWEDEN IS IN FLAMES TONIGHT, AS PALESTINIANS, BASQUE SEPARATISTS, IRISH REPUBLICANS, QUEBECOIS, HOPI INDIANS, AND EVERY OTHER NATIONALIST GROUP SEEKING A HOMELAND TRIES TO STAKE A CLAIM TO THIS RULER-LESS LAND.
ANITA'S
EK-BURGER
STOCKHOLM ZOO
ULLMAN'S ALMONDS

AS THE HOME OF THE NOBEL PEACE PRIZE CRUMBLES IN AN ORGY OF VIOLENCE, THE QUESTION ON EVERYONE'S MIND IS THE SAME--WHERE, OH WHERE, IS WAYLON SMITHERS?
OH, I THINK I KNOW WHERE HE IS...

I'M HUNGRY. AND IT SMELLS LIKE CAT FOOD IN HERE. AND I'M MISSING "DIAGNOSIS MURDER."
THE END

THE TEN COMMANDMENTS

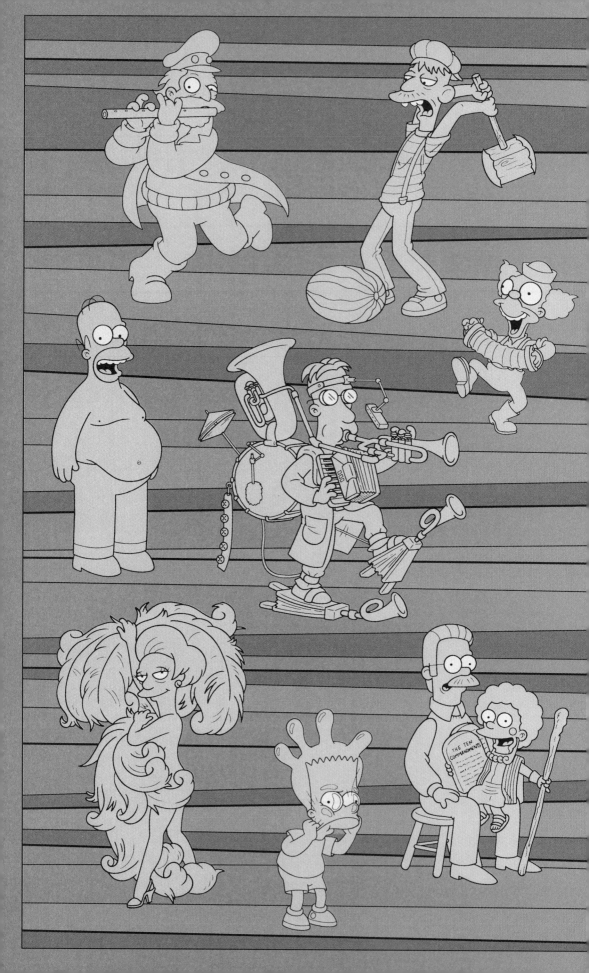